The ... Peterson

by: RJ PARKER

"This is a work of nonfiction. No names have been changed, no characters invented, no events fabricated."

RJ Parker

The Staircase

The Murder of Kathleen Peterson

by: RJ PARKER

ISBN-13: 978-1725558830
ISBN-10: 1725558831

Copyright and Published

by *RJ Parker Publishing*

Published in United States of America

Copyrights

This book is licensed for your personal enjoyment only. All rights reserved. No part of this publication can be reproduced or transmitted in any form or by any means without prior written authorization from *RJ Parker Publishing*. The unauthorized reproduction or distribution of a copyrighted work is illegal. Criminal copyright infringement, including infringement without monetary gain, is investigated by the FBI and is punishable by fines and federal imprisonment.

Table of Contents

Monthly KINDLE HD FIRE Giveaway..................7
Introduction..8
Background/Personal Life....................................10
As a Novelist...17
Relationship with Patricia....................................21
Kathleen Peterson...23
Jury Selection and Openings................................36
Prosecution's Case..41
Michael's Benefits from Wife's Death 44
Defense's Case..58
    Defense Team Raises 10 Reasons Why Michael Peterson Wouldn't Have Killed Kathleen..............79
The Jury Deliberates...85
The Verdict...88
The Owl or the Husband: Who's the Real Culprit? 92
Deaver Convinced Jurors About Michael's Conviction..101
Retrial Hearing..105
Peterson accepts an Alford Plea..........................111
Conspiracy Theories About The Death Of Kathleen Peterson..113
Interesting Staircase Facts about Michael and Kathleen Peterson...119
Where are Michael and His Family Now?..........123
Epilogue..126
FREE BOOK..127
    ABDUCTION: The Minivan Murders............127
Introduction..127
Biography...130
Michelle Michaud...142
Spree of Terror...153

The Events of December 2, 1997............................170
The Investigation and Arrest...............................178
Trial and Further Details......................................186
Sentencing..199
A Psychological Profile.......................................203
Appreciation...218
Books by RJ Parker..219
About the Author...221
Contact Information...222

Monthly KINDLE HD FIRE Giveaway

***

Drawing each month on the 30th...

***

Enter to WIN
(No Purchase Necessary)

Click HERE   http://rjpp.ca/KINDLE

Introduction

Love. Affection. Romance. Happiness. Care. Kids. Beauty. Trust. Belief -- these are some of the other names when describing the relationship of a husband and wife. Both partners are responsible to make the world beautiful for each other. Whether it's about sharing duties or enjoying the moments, one is incomplete without the other. Or, we can say that the world is nothing if one goes away because there is no one who could take that special person's place.

But what happens when one spouse decides to eliminate the other? What would happen if one decides to live the rest of his/her life with someone else, or alone? That is the time when feelings die and the relationship has no better option but separation. But guess what, if they do have children, *they* would be the real victims since they have to decide with whom they want to live!

This happened with Todd and Clayton Peterson when their parents, Michael and Patricia Peterson, separated. Although they were happy, something went wrong in their relationship which caused them to go their separate ways. Luckily, Michael found a new partner in Kathleen Atwater, and they were married after dating for some time. Or, unlucky for Kathleen.

Their lives changed when Kathleen

Peterson was found dead on the staircase of their Durham mansion. Everything changed. Police claimed that it was a murder and Michael was the prime suspect. (The spouse is usually the number one suspect in any domestic homicide.)

So read this true crime story and get to know about how Michael dealt with the trial, what the evidence was and lacked that found him guilty of murder, and where he is right now. The book is full of interesting plots and twists that actually happened throughout the proceedings.

Background/Personal Life

Michael Peterson is now in his mid-seventies. He lives a quiet life in Durham, North Carolina, and maintains relationships with his two biological children, Clayton and Todd, and their adopted siblings, Margaret and Martha. Most of the rest of his family is estranged.

Michael was born in Nashville, Tennessee, on October 23, 1943, to Eugene (or Eugen) Iver Peterson and Eleanor Peterson nee Bartolino. Michael had one brother, Jack. Eugene was a career military officer, and the family moved frequently. Traveling encouraged Michael to become an avid reader. He hoped to become a celebrated author in the tradition of his favorite author, Ernest Hemingway.

A student of political science at Duke University, Michael was involved in campus activities. He edited the student newspaper, *The Chronicle,* and was president of Sigma Nu Fraternity. He graduated in 1965 and briefly attended law school at the University of North Carolina at Chapel Hill.

In 1965, Michael first got married to Patricia Sue in Durham where she used to teach at an elementary school of the Rhein-Main Air Base near Frankfurt, West Germany. They were blessed with two sons, Clayton and Todd. While living in Germany, the Petersons became close friends with Elizabeth and

George Ratliff and their two children, Margaret and Martha. After George died, Elizabeth relied on the Petersons for emotional support. Then, in 1985, Elizabeth died after falling down the stairs in her home in Grafenhausen, and Michael became guardian of the two girls.

Patricia and Michael divorced in 1987. The reasons were unknown, and the couple maintained a congenial relationship after their divorce. Martha and Margaret continued to live with Michael. Clayton and Todd stayed with their mother at first, then moved in with Michael and the girls who had moved to Durham, North Carolina.

Kathleen Hunt Atwater was a neighbor of the Petersons in Durham. Ten years his junior, Kathleen was a leader and prominent citizen in Durham. A divorced mother of one daughter, Caitlin, Kathleen was an executive at Nortel Networks where she received awards for leadership. She traveled for her work to Russia, Ukraine, Vietnam, Malaysia, Europe, Hong Kong, and Canada.

Michael met Kathleen through their children. Caitlin was friends with Martha and Margaret and was thrilled when in 1989, Michael and the children moved in with Kathleen and Caitlin. They were married in 1997. At that time, they lived in a home on Bull City Rising described as being over 9,000 square feet and sitting on 3.5 acres of land. The home had five bedrooms and six bathrooms, plenty of room for the family. Later on, they moved to a Durham mansion of 11,000 square feet with their five children. The family tree of Michael was a bit complicated since it comprises of a lot of people who were not related to him directly.

Caitlin Atwater: Michael's stepdaughter, who was worried about her mother getting married with someone she already knew. She was a friend of Martha and Margaret and, therefore, was feeling a bit confused about her relationship after Michael and Kathleen married. She was very happy when Michael and Kathleen got married since she found nothing but love and affection in their relationship.

Clayton Peterson: Elder son of Patricia and Michael who used to live with Michael after his parents got divorced. He believed that his father was innocent of Kathleen's murder.

Todd Peterson: Second son from Michael's first wife who was always there for Michael's support.

Margaret Ratliff: One of the adopted daughters of George and Elizabeth Ratliff. She also believed that her new father didn't do anything.

Martha Ratliff: Sister of Margaret and a supporter of Michael.

Although Michael was an admitted bisexual who reportedly had repeated sexual encounters with men throughout their marriage, the children said the marriage was a happy one and the Petersons were excellent parents. After Kathleen's death, Michael was reported as saying, *"Kathleen was my life, I whispered her name in my heart a thousand times, she is there but I can't stop crying."*

The Petersons did have family issues. Clayton Peterson had turbulent teenage years in Germany. He moved to Durham to be with his father, planning to attend Duke University. At the age of 19, however, he was arrested and subsequently convicted of planting a pipe bomb submerged in gasoline in a Duke University administrative office. He admitted to the crime and said he had done it to divert attention from his simultaneous theft of photo identification equipment to make a fake ID.

After serving time in prison, Clayton enrolled in North Carolina State University where he became class valedictorian.

Todd Clayton also graduated from NCSU and worked briefly at Nortel Networks, his stepmother's employer. He left, however, to start a website called Futazi.com. The site was a message board for teenagers and offered advice on dating, kissing, sexuality, and friendship. It also had photos of scantily clad high school girls. Todd had an alter ego on this site named "Roman Croft". Croft was a bodybuilder, and the site showed "before" and "after" photos of him in boxer shorts.

The Petersons were active members of the Durham community and, in 1999, Michael ran for Mayor of Durham. He was soundly defeated after questions arose about his credibility. Peterson had served in Vietnam. He claimed several awards including the Bronze Star with Valor and two Purple Hearts. He had no paperwork to back up his medals and later admitted he had received a Purple Heart and Honorable Discharge after a car accident in Japan.

There are signs that the apparently happy Peterson marriage may have been strained. Despite a supposed net worth of over $2 million, they had over $140,000 in credit card debt in 2001. When Martha Ratliff was slated to attend the University of San Francisco, a private college costing $33,000 per year, Michael contacted Martha's paternal uncle to assist with $5,000 each semester. The uncle agreed.

In November 2001, Michael contacted his ex-wife, Patricia, requesting she take out a loan for $30,000 to pay off credit card debt incurred by their sons, Clayton and Todd. Reportedly, he told Patricia that he couldn't discuss the issue with Kathleen.

As to Michael Peterson's bisexuality, it is unclear whether Kathleen knew about his relationships and agreed to them. Michael had at least one confirmed email relationship with a male escort. They had plans to meet in person, but the escort stood him up.

Peterson had served in Vietnam and later wrote several books inspired by his military career and his career in government service. He also worked as a newspaper columnist and became known for his strong political views and his criticism of Durham police and County District Attorney James Hardin Jr. Hardin was to play a much larger role in Peterson's future.

Michael Peterson's future is what this book is about. There are those who would say that Peterson is an intelligent, patriotic, and loving man. Others would say he is a self-involved narcissist with a grandiose sense of self-importance. Perhaps he is both, perhaps neither.

As a Novelist

As an alumnus of Duke University, a veteran of the Vietnamese Marine Corps and, most importantly, a renowned novelist, Michael Peterson was among those people who always remained in the highlights. Before starting to write novels, he was an active and major contributor in the Marine Corps and served with his best for a significant time period. He fought many wars and battles against the enemies and learned a lot about the conflicts between the parties.

Michael, the son of Eugen, received his Bachelor degree in political science from Duke University but, his thirst for education and dedication to learn about law, took him to Chapel Hill, North Carolina's Law School. After completing his education, in 1968, Michael took on his responsibilities in the US Marines Corps. Truth be told, his career life had been full of controversies. He was particularly known for serving during the Vietnam War because he was a person who got permanently disabled due to a car accident in Japan. He fought from that level and regained his confidence to restart his life. With incredible services and efforts, he was honorably given the rank of a Captain, he also claimed a Bronze Star, Silver Star and two purple hearts. But, there was no documentation of his claims.

After he left the Marine Corps, Michael

found his interest in book writing and decided to share his experience in Vietnam. Michael started to list down points and ultimately wrote three books in which he discussed different wars and events he came across throughout his service. He became famous as a novelist due to three novels, namely A Time of War, The Enemy, and The Immortal Dragon, because they were the perfect representation of what he had gone through. These novels discussed everything about the Vietnamese conflict. All three novels were in handwritten form, which were later printed and published officially.

His experience as an Editor of The Duke Chronicle, the student newspaper at Duke University, also helped a lot to make everything work just the right way. Michael was also the co-writer of the Marines of Love Company and the Biographical Charlie Two Shoes with David Perlmutt, the journalist. He also worked for the Durham Herald-Sun as a newspaper columnist. He used to highlight and criticize the Durham police for their inabilities, due to which his columns captured most of the attention and he become popular over time.

After combining the impact, outcomes and experiences of his past life, Michael started a new chapter of his life and began to deliver his thoughts to others. Instead of returning home from the Vietnam War and trying to forget everything, he brought everything on the papers and wrote these detailed, interesting and inspiring novels.

1. *Immortal Dragon*

Finalized and published in 1983, Immortal Dragon is the beginning of Michael's services in the Marine Corps during the Vietnam War. The novel is the perfect representation of what had actually happened during the war. It focuses on the 19th century events when Andre Lafabre came from France to Vietnam in disguise and was caught up in deadly intrigues. He struggled for power and made all efforts to regain his status.

2. *A Time of War*

Published in 1990, this novel is the continuation to his experience in Vietnam. The novelist captures the essence of time. Michael Peterson has written this astounding and richly-textured novel with incredible creativity and knowledge. He discusses the classical story of Vietnam that is blood-chilling, brilliant, compelling and sweeping.

3. *A Bitter Peace*

This sequel of Michael Peterson's war classic about Vietnam revolves around the Presidential thoughts over Bradley Marshall's mission for regaining peace with honor in the country. But unluckily, things did not turn out in the way they are expected, and his efforts turned into failure that would haunt him for years. This novel is full of unremitting suspense and wrenching insight over how a man seeks to achieve his goals and deals with personal redemption.

4. *Charlie Two Shoes and the Marines of Love Company*

Michael co-worked on this novel with David Perlmutt and brought this masterpiece to limelight in 1998. This novel is about an 11-year old Chinese boy, named Tsui Chi-Hsii, who is famous as Charlie Tsuii, his American name. He was approached by a company of US Marines which was transferred to China in 1945 right after World War II ends. He was intended to protect the men of Love Company, from 1st Division, in return for clothing and food. The Marine Division also took the responsibility of his education, but as the communists took charge of China in 1949, Charlie was left alone as the Love Company had to leave the country. Charlie had to suffer and struggle to make both ends meet in China.

While looking at the facts, it's quite evident to say that Michael's popularity as a novelist is still unclear due to his conviction in 2001 for the murder of his second wife, Kathleen Peterson. However, his efforts for Charlie Two Shoes explain the extent of his skills on their own. The way he converted this real-life story into a thrilling and exciting masterpiece is quite remarkable. Even the collection of three books on the Vietnam War is something that readers could not forget and would love to read again and again.

Relationship with Patricia

The relationship of a husband with his wife is one of the most beautiful and trusted realities; that no one could deny. Being a supporting wife of a hard-working husband is what makes the bonding of Michael Peterson and Patricia Sue Peterson stronger. As the famous quote says: *"A man's success is measured by what his wife and children say about him. Money and accomplishments mean nothing if you let your home fail."*

The same goes for Michael Peterson and his family where his first wife used to support him at every stage of life. Even his children had been quite supportive and cooperative. Patricia Peterson was among those women who were always present with their husband.

Whether it was about helping him to write novels or increasing morale to fight against life problems, Patricia had been of great support to Michael Peterson. After their marriage in 1965, the couple was living a beautiful life and received the world's greatest blessings in the form of Todd and Clayton. The family was having a great time together until 1987 when the couple divorced.

After their separation, Michael was performing his responsibilities as the guardian of Martha and Margaret (daughters of his neighbors in Germany, George and Elizabeth

Ratliff) while Todd and Clayton were living with Patricia.

After almost ten years, in 1997, Michael Peterson married Kathleen and began living in Cedar Street Home in Norwalk, California USA. Kathleen also had a daughter named Caitlin. After some time, there were joined by Todd and Clayton, and the extended family started with new aspirations and intentions to live their lives.

Yet, Patricia had a soft spot for Michael due to which she and her sons had been a huge support for Michael when he was convicted of murdering his second wife, Kathleen. She even took part in the hearing and had a clear stance that Michael couldn't do anything like that. After living so many years with him, she was quite certain he was innocent and would say that she had believed in him and would until her last breath.

Patricia was even certain about Michael and Kathleen's relationship as husband and wife. At one occasion, she said that she knew everything about their married life and was quite happy to see them together. Although they hardly talked with each other, their bond with the children was as strong and trustworthy as it should be.

Kathleen Peterson

After being separated from Patricia in 1987, Michael began to live alone and had focused on his career more than before. He became quite serious about what he was doing. He dedicated many years to himself and tried to explore new opportunities in order to pursue his career accordingly. After living alone for a few years, he met Kathleen Hunt Atwater who was a widow and mother of a girl named Caitlin Atwater. They became really good friends and showed complete interest in each other.

Kathleen was born on February 21, 1953, in Greensboro, North Carolina. Kathleen was quite a dedicated and enthusiastic individual about her dreams and initially decided to complete her studies in engineering while she also showed incredible leadership qualities. Since Michael was, himself, a successful and career-oriented person, he was inspired by Kathleen's professional journey from her school to college. He used to appreciate her for being an active contributor at school, where she performed her responsibilities as the President of the Debating Club along with fulfilling her duties as an Editor for the 'Generation' school magazine.

Kathleen received her BS degree in civil engineering and pursued her Master's in mechanical engineering from Duke University.

Michael and Kathleen were quite identical with respect to their dedication towards making their careers successful and brighter. Kathleen received many leadership awards while Michael was a renowned fiction novelist.

They were married in 1997 and moved in at 1810 Cedar Street, a suburb of Durham in North Carolina. The 48-year-old woman was living her life to the fullest and was working a perfect job at Nortel as a Business Executive, while her personal life was also doing great. However, for her, the real accomplishment was her family, which she created and raised with a lot of love and affection. Kathleen always had complete support from her love and best friend Michael, along with their children, Caitlin, Todd, Clayton, Margaret and Martha. Even Kathleen's mother in Florida (Veronica Hunt), sisters living in Virginia (Lori Campbell and Candace Zamperini) and brother in Tennessee (Steven Hunt) were also there to help and support her.

*****

The Petersons were living an above-average life. Their 11,000-square-foot mansion is the masterpiece of Chinese trinkets and artwork, particularly their huge living room that shows off their style sense and knowledge about how to incorporate antique items into their home.

Bright sunlight streams into the rooms

from amazingly installed bay windows that is reflected by glass-covered photographs of Kathleen and Michael's wedding. Everything in their three-story mansion seems to be in complete harmony with the surroundings.

Their life was going so simple and enjoyable with their five children that they never thought of becoming the subject of one of the most mysterious and baffling true crime stories, featured as '*The Staircase Murders.*'

*****

During the early hours of December 9, 2001, Kathleen Peterson was found dead on the blood-stained staircase of their mansion. The evidence on the hardwood floor boards and salmon-colored walls explained the entire story of how badly she had fallen. The amount of blood on the staircase seemed to be quite inconsistent, which was giving a different impression from what had been told to the police initially. Even the actual and confirmed time of death was different from what Michael told the 911 operator. The investigators also uncovered extramarital dalliances and referred to the similarities between Kathleen's death and another stairway fall of their close friend's wife. These initial discoveries were pointing to Michael as the major suspect since there was so much deviation between his statements and the actual findings.

Aphrodite Jones wrote a book on Michael's role as the husband, titled '*A Perfect*

Husband,' in which Michael talked about a case that was similar to what happened to Kathleen that night. In that case, the battle led to some legal allegations that turned out to be one of the longest proceedings in Tennessee history. The same excerpts were found in the Kathleen Peterson death case when some strong evidences pointed to Michael for manipulating information. His call to 911 was suspicious as if he was trying to cover his role in her death. However, there was another perception that he was shocked and scared after seeing his wife that way and, therefore, he said whatever came in his mind first.

*****

It was 2:40 AM on December 9, 2001, when a frantic and shocked man dialed 911 to ask for help in an emergency. He was breathing heavily while reporting the incident to Durham police in North Carolina that his wife fell down the stairs at their Cedar Street home. The caller reported that she had an accident and was still breathing. Their conversation after reporting the crime is as follows:

9-1-1 Operator: Okay, how many stairs did she fall down?

Caller: What? Huh?

9-1-1 Operator: How many stairs?

Caller: Stairs?

9-1-1 Operator: How many stairs?

Caller: Ah . . . Oh . . .

9-1-1 Operator: Calm down, sir. Calm down.

According to the operator, the caller was really confused and kept saying that his wife was unconscious. He was asking for the emergency crew to arrive with help immediately. He provided the address, but the operator was a bit unsure about how to calm him down. She was having difficulty in understanding what he was saying. He was breathing hard while his voice was so shrill that it was hard to understand a single word. She assured him that help would be there within a few minutes. He just had to calm down and answer some important questions:

9-1-1 Operator: Calm down, sir. Calm down. How many stairs did she fall down?

Caller: Oh, fifteen, twenty. I don't know. Please get somebody here right away. Please!

9-1-1 Operator: Sir, somebody else is dispatching the ambulance.

Caller: It's in Forest Hills, okay? Please! Please!

9-1-1- Operator: Okay. Is she awake now? Hello? Hello?

There was no reply from the caller, but she could hear him yelling '*Oh God!*' in the background, and then, no connection! The operator immediately dialed Engine 5, Medic 5 to alert the emergency crew. She directly transferred information to the rescue team and sent them to the Cedar Street home address. As soon as she completed her radio call with the team, there was another emergency call ringing on 911.

9-1-1 Operator: Durham 911, what is your emergency?

Caller: Where are they? Why is she not breathing? Please! Please, would you hurry up!

The caller was able to hear a static voice from the background as if someone was talking with the radio operators and yelling Code 5. The caller was getting frantic with every passing second, but there was no reply to the operator's words:

9-1-1 Operator: Sir? Hello? Hello?

Eight minutes later, the rescue team was able to find the place on Cedar Street because they took a wrong turn in the wooded neighborhood. All the lights in the house were on that time, and the paramedics immediately rushed into the home and found the victim on the stairs. She had no pulse.

Officers Figueroa and McDowell from Durham Police Department soon arrived at the scene and began their investigation. Police then went ahead and attempted to identify the caller, but he was so shocked and hysterical that he wasn't able to control himself from crying.

What Officers Said About the Scene

According to Officer Figueroa, as he arrived at the Cedar Street Home, it was 2:50 A.M. and everything seemed to be quite mysterious and troublesome. The victim, Kathleen Atwater Peterson, was lying at the bottom of the stairs in a pool of blood with her head against the stairwell. There were also male athletic shoes beside her with a pair of flip-flop sandals and white socks. What caught the officer's attention was the roll of paper towels soaked in blood.

At 3:07 A.M., Figueroa was joined by

Dan George, Durham Investigator, along with other patrol cars and fire trucks which were sent to inspect the back entryway to the residence. George intentionally walked through the scene and instructed Figueroa to secure the residence before moving on with his investigation. Since the mansion was quite huge, they asked for more backup in order to cover the entire space within a short time period. On his initial analysis, he reported that there was blood everywhere, especially on the walls and several steps leading to the stairway. Both officers waited until the Crime Investigation Department (CID) reached the place.

As soon as he met the investigation team, George mentioned that there was something wrong with the scene. Following his lead, the investigation team began following the evidence and headed to the kitchen door where Michael Peterson was standing, dressed in a T-shirt and shorts. He was also covered in blood. His son Todd was also present behind him as he was trying to console Michael. He was constantly mentioning to check Kathleen's body. Just a few minutes later, Michael rushed towards his wife, bent down, cried and caressed her. His actions were so immediate that no officer had a chance to prevent him from touching her body and probably further contaminating the questionable crime scene.

After trying on their own with no results, they asked Todd to help his father move away from her body. But, unfortunately, the damage was already done and the evidence was not there in the actual form. Michael managed to transfer bloodstains on his body as well, thus making it more difficult for forensics.

Not only such actions made him suspicious, but Dan George also noticed a civilian, a young lady named Christina Tomasetti, the daughter of Michael's best friend. George questioned her presence in the kitchen. Christina stated that she was with Todd at a party and had just arrived when the fire trucks reached the crime scene.

As soon as the officers followed the instructions to seal the scene, two more people, Ben Maynard and Heather Whitson, approached from out of nowhere. They had been called by Todd for help because they were in the neighborhood. Todd specifically told Ben to bring Heather because she was a medical student at Duke University and knew how to help his father to come out of shock.

As they arrived at the scene, Durham Police were not likely to let them enter the home but, upon Todd's request, they eventually allowed them to enter. Todd took them around the staircase and entered into the kitchen through the fine dining room. All of them consoled Mr. Peterson and made all efforts to take him out of the trauma. But nothing was working as he couldn't bear the pain of such a big loss, his wife. He refused to accept any medical care and wanted to be left alone.

Michael kept mumbling that he couldn't live without his beloved wife! He recapped the entire day of December 9, 2001:

Michael and Kathleen were enjoying a few drinks as part of their celebration.

They were having a great time together.

Michael, then, went towards the pool area and took the dogs to spend some time with them as well.

He thought that Kathleen was upstairs going to bed, but never thought of seeing something like that.

Considering his father's grief and sadness, Todd asked the uniformed officers if he could take a look at his stepmom's body a bit closer. They granted him permission to do so, and as he knelt down, he touched her legs and found no signs of life. Then, with the help of a flashlight, everyone paid attention to Kathleen's injured head and found something wrong at the blood around her body and clothes. As well, there were bruises and a strange pained look on her face.

According to the Witness, Fran Borden:

As soon as he arrived at the 1810 Cedar Street home on December 9, 2001, Sergeant Borden was instructed to investigate a woman's death who was reported to have fallen down the staircase. Upon his arrival, his attention was caught by the blood stains on a kitchen cabinet and a drawer handle. As per his later statement to the jurors, that was the *'first of the three red flags'*.

The second flag was the amount of blood present around and on the victim who was lying at the bottom of a staircase. There was a lot of blood. The third and last red flag was the position of the victim's body which seemed to be in a perfect alignment with respect to the spine and head. The reason behind his suspicion was that her position shouldn't be that way if she had fallen from any amount of steps. During his interview, Borden said:

"*I squatted in the stairwell and looked up the stairs, trying to visualize every possible scenario how this woman could have come down those stairs, landed in the position where she landed, and, where did all that blood come from?*"

After listening to his words, the prosecution witness immediately responded by saying that that's not all he had mentioned. But defense lawyers claimed that there were more facts Borden didn't talk about. They brought attention to the reality that the blood could have been transferred by Todd when he received permission from the investigating officers to sit near the dead body of his stepmom. Borden, then, immediately responded: *"That information could have been helpful. I did not have it."*

The defense lawyer also questioned the credibility of the only witness, Borden, who already knew that Mr. Peterson used to criticize Durham Police for being incompetent and unprofessional. During Peterson's time period as the columnist from 1998 to 1999, he wrote many newspaper columns sarcastically, claiming that local criminals were actually smarter and more efficient than the police because they didn't know how to do their work.

There are numerous hidden facts and details involved in this murder that might contribute to making a certain decision. Michael was arrested when suspicion was supported by some strong evidence, and his innocence was questioned in many forms. The case was, therefore, brought in the front of the local court for trial.

Jury Selection and Openings

Cases of murder that go through a long trial are hardly uncomplicated. The Peterson case, however, has so many contending issues that his single count murder case trial could run up to three months and even more.

For seven weeks plus, a rigorous selection process for the twelve members of the jury and an additional four alternates were carried out. Their purpose would be to ascertain if the prosecuting team possessed enough testimony and proof to charge Mr. Peterson of murder, or to figure out the contradictory testimony given by the experts, who would also be speaking in the course of the coming weeks, on whether Kathleen Peterson's demise a year and six months ago was premeditated or accidental.

The case had made headlines so many times in North Carolina, right from the time the prosecuting attorneys stated they believed Michael Peterson, who had now turned 59, had murdered his wife, Kathleen.

Some police officials and the emergency medical team who made their way to the Peterson's home that night were of the opinion that Kathleen Peterson tripped from the steps of the staircase and fractured her head when it hit the wall. But again, there was blood all over the stairway area, the walls, the steps of the staircase, and also all around Michael's clothes, which seemed to suggest otherwise to the officers from the Durham unit.

The suspicion of the detectives was further aroused after an autopsy was carried out. The examiners found deep cuts and five outstanding lesions which they reasoned caused her to bleed to death.

Todd Peterson, Michael's son from his first marriage, said, "*It is simply unimaginable; my father and Kathleen had a very amiable and peaceful life together. They never had any major argument.*"

In the courtroom, when the hearing commenced, Todd would be seated right behind his father and the defense counsel, David Rudolf and Thomas Maher. And with Todd would be his sisters, Martha and Margaret Ratliff. Also present was Caitlin Atwater, Kathleen's daughter from a previous marriage, who was accusing Michael Peterson and had severed her relationship with Michael's sons and the Ratliff sisters.

The incident occurred at a time when only Kathleen and Michael were in the mansion, the prosecuting counsel would argue. Her injuries alone didn't seem to be inflicted from an accidental fall down the stairway, as claimed by the defense team. Furthermore, if the judge obliged them during objections, they would probably hold on to the similar occurrence with Elizabeth Ratliff back in 1985, where Peterson was the last person seen leaving the house by a neighbor.

According to Peterson, as spoken through his lawyers, he and Kathleen had drinks outside their home by the swimming pool on Saturday night, after which she headed inside alone, so she must have either fainted or tripped on the stairs as the stairway was dimly lit, which led to her hitting her head and ultimately bleeding to death.

David Rudolf, reputed to be among the renowned lawyers in North Carolina, would draw attention to the fact that there was no murder weapon, eyewitness or striking motive. He would be employing the services of experts in disputing the forensic analysis presented by the opposing side's witnesses, which would include Dr. Henry Lee, a forensic scientist of repute. David would also challenge that there were no regular traces of blood patterns around the staircase, as expected when a person is continuously hit with a blunt object.

Hardin said to the members of the jury on commencement of the long-awaited trial, "*The deceased was most likely hit with a blow poke which practically disappeared into thin air as it cannot be traced.*" Sentencing Peterson to life imprisonment would require Hardin to prove, firstly, that Kathleen's life was ended intentionally, and secondly, that the heinous crime was committed by her husband, Michael.

David Rudolf stated that the prosecution team was narrow minded in choosing to label

Michael a suspect. Subsequent to deterring him from attending his wife's wake while they carried out a search at his home, the prosecution team also hurriedly assembled a grand jury before Christmas in 2001. In a couple of hours, they had the warrant they required to put Peterson behind bars all through the holidays.

The investigation proceeded better only after the arraignment, David said. He made note of the fact that the opposing team made no attempt to collect Michael's financial reports until May 5th, following the start of the selection of members of the jury. The prosecuting attorneys were of the opinion that Michael Peterson could have wanted his wife dead for monetary reasons.

Rudolf pointed out that the records would reveal that the net worth of the Petersons was almost $2 million and that Michael was required to split a life insurance policy of $1.4 million with his stepdaughter.

"They weren't moved by money. They enjoyed it, but it wasn't all that for them," said Rudolf.

Rudolf also accused the police officials of wanting to settle a score with Peterson simply because he had penned a number of articles in several newspapers condemning the police. In one of them, Peterson said that the police department of Durham was the most terrible in unraveling crimes in North Carolina.

In another one, he wrote -- as if he saw the future -- "*The probability of capturing a criminal is just a little bit higher than being struck by lightning.*"

While members of the jury were being selected, some panelists said that they knew of the report of the death of Elizabeth Ratliff, who was 43 years old and a schoolteacher. She was a close friend of Michael Peterson and Patricia, his first wife, while they all resided in Germany.

Elizabeth Ratliff **Kathleen Peterson**
Stair accident **Stair accident**
died 1985 **died 2001**

Accident?

Prosecution's Case

Wet or Dry? Blood's State is Questionable

During the murder case of Kathleen Peterson, a medical assistant revealed he had never seen so much blood in his life until he saw Kathleen's body. Michael Peterson's defense counsel strove to upturn any harm the opposing team's first witness might have caused to their case. James Rose, the medical assistant, testified on how he and his partner on duty rushed down to the crime scene when they were called on December 9, 2001, at 3:00 AM. The caller was Michael who reported that his wife had tripped on the stairs and had severe injuries.

Rose, one of the EMT paramedics, addressed the jury, saying, "*It's quite weird for us to find so much blood from a fall.*"

During cross-examination, Thomas Maher, one of the defense lawyers, proceeded to explain to the jurors that Rose was inexperienced with severe fall situations, saying he had only been called for one which didn't involve a tipsy victim.

The defense team pitched their tent on the premise that Kathleen tripped on the steps of the staircase because, firstly, it was dimly lit, and, two, that she had drunk champagne and wine. The opposing counsel argued that the fall couldn't have led to so much bleeding and seven lesions on her head; therefore, she must have been hit severely and repeatedly on her head with an object.

Following an intense hearing in the absence of the jury, Judge Orlando Hudson asked that the jury disregard the medical assistant's testimony, saying the victim was already dead about 30 minutes prior to the arrival of the ambulance.

David Rudolf, with the defense, questioned Rose's experience with forensic pathology, saying his probable guess of how long Kathleen had been dead wasn't valid, as it could still occur medically even if the victim were alive.

James Rose testified further, saying:

Michael was pretty discomposed when they arrived and couldn't answer simple questions, such as the victim's birth date;

The entrance door was ajar as the ambulance arrived at 2.48 AM, and he noticed two drops of blood just before the entrance door;

Michael said he had gone to switch off the lights by the pool, only to return indoors and find Kathleen at the base of the stairs. This countered Peterson's earlier statement of saying he was back outside until 30 to 45 minutes after his wife went inside.

Rose stated during cross-examination

that his first statement to the police didn't include drying of blood or Peterson switching off the lights by the pool. He did, however, mention both in his second statement to the police three days after the death.

Another medical assistant, Ron Paige, said it was obvious Kathleen was dead when he looked closely at the stairway area. Her eyes were wide open and blood was on her head, on the wall, floor and even on Michael.

"Michael stood above Kathleen's body crying. Seemed like he wanted to help her, I can't say for sure. But he had blood all over him, which seemed to be dried up."

When questioned by the defense team, Paige agreed he didn't touch Michael to ascertain whether the blood was dried or still wet, and he didn't mention about the blood seeming dry in his statement to the police on the night of the incident.

Michael's Benefits from Wife's Death

On July 3, 2003 -- almost six months after Kathleen's death -- Michael Peterson has claimed her 401k pension and savings plan – up to $347, 000, the jury was told.

Coming in on day number three of Peterson's case, the pecuniary evidence was a move by the opposing team to prove that Peterson had something to gain monetarily from his wife's demise.

Jim Hardin Jr., Durham's D.A., stated to the jury in his opening remarks that Michael was entitled to part of Kathleen's life insurance fund of $1.4 million if he's able to avoid life imprisonment and can win any case leveled against him concerning that by Kathleen's first husband and her daughter.

A staff member in the Human Resources department at Kathleen's work place, Katherine Kayser, testified that Peterson received $94,455 from Kathleen's pension plan on February 11, 2002. He also received $29,360 one week earlier from her 401k retirement plan. At the end of May that year, Peterson had garnered a total of $223,00 from three payments, all from Kathleen's deferred compensation plan.

On counter examination, defense counsel, Thomas Maher, using personnel records from Nortel Network, argued that

Kathleen's worth was more as a living being than if she was dead.

If she were still alive, Kathleen's $145,000 per annum would have been ongoing. She would also still have her 401k account and pension plans increasing, not forgetting ongoing receipt of stock options. He also pointed out that Peterson and his children had already lost the health insurance benefits attached to Kathleen's job.

Going by the current stock prices at that time, Maher pointed out that Kathleen could earn a total of $677,000 in 2001 if she sold 22,600 units of stock which she had had since 1994.

At the close of court, prior to a weekend holiday, David Rudolf explained to CourtTV.com that there was nothing wrong with Peterson seeking Kathleen's benefits in January 2002. He posted an $850,000 bond for his bail consequent to his indictment that same month.

On July 8, 2003, Jayson Crank, a firefighter in Durham, told the jury he noticed what was probably dried blood right at the entrance door of the Peterson's home. Being the fourth to testify of such, dried blood became a major issue. The opposing team's conviction is that Peterson killed his wife and then called 911 to say his wife had tripped on the staircase.

The jury witnessed testimony for the prosecuting team from Raymond Young, who said the Petersons were spending about $100,000 in excess of their income three years consecutively, prior to the passing of Kathleen at the age of 48.

Bringing forth a probable pecuniary motive very early in the trial, the prosecutors seemed to be withholding their physical evidence. Forensic handlers would be testifying that Kathleen's head wounds and blood spatter can be more likened to that of a beating rather than to a fall.

A former co-employee of Kathleen at Nortel also testified, saying that the deceased sounded normal when they spoke on the phone just a few hours before the incident.

Helen Prislinger, a witness from Ontario, Canada, took the stand on the summons of the prosecutors and said she and Kathleen spoke earlier about Nortel's current issues, and nothing seemed odd about her household that particular night.

Prosecuting Team Emphasized over the Blood Spatter Evidence

July 21, 2003 – Though very stressful, the evidence that heralded the fourth week of Peterson's trial was necessary for the prosecuting team to set things up for the pathologist and blood spatter expert, both of whom would be very crucial in their case against Peterson.

Dan George, a crime scene technician with the police, was on the stand for the second time, spotting evidence materials he garnered along with his colleagues on the night and in the next days after the incident. George, one of the most important witnesses in the trial, told the jury he collected items such as clothes, watches, hair, blood, computers, wine glasses, cups, shoes, etc. from the Petersons. The need to identify the items was critical because subsequent witnesses would need it to deduce what actually happened on the dimly lit stairway that night.

George, during interrogation, stated he didn't hold on to the three bloody paper towels recovered from underneath the head of the victim; neither did he withhold a blood-stained telephone. It wasn't long after Peterson's defense team commenced the cross examination of George that the court had to take a recess, but it was certain that the defense team would be harnessing the testimony to their advantage. They would base it on the shortcomings of the police, which would render arguable the blood spatter analysis.

David Rudolf took a lot of time in examining George's hypothesis that Michael took a knife from the kitchen and sat beside Kathleen's dead body before the emergency team arrived.

On July 22, 2003, apart from not collecting the household items with blood stains, George also did not take a photo of the bloody footprints lined up in the Peterson's kitchen, which were only obvious on application of luminol, and the findings weren't penned in his first report.

"Don't you think that was a vital finding to note, if you had visualized it?" Rudolf asked. *"I agree, sir, it was, but three other police officers witnessed it."*

Rudolf went further to question George's competence when he pointed to an inconsistency in his earlier statement. George had been asked, during a hearing before the trial began in March, why he avoided taking photos of the chemical reaction, and he had replied, "*I'm unable to answer that.*"

The prosecuting team had implied indirectly that Peterson paced around their kitchen with his bare feet but cleaned up all signs before proceeding to dial 911 to say his spouse had tripped on the flight of stairs.

George, during interrogation, accepted that Michael paced the house with bare feet while the officers were obtaining all the evidence they could obtain within the early hours of December 9, 2001.

The blood spatter expert was now ready to be questioned by the defense. Peterson's counsel were very ready to discredit his results, and whatever they wanted to deduce from it. The opposing team were banking on the conclusions from the blood spatter expert to drive home their stand that Peterson beat his wife to death but made it seem like she fell. The defense, on the other hand, were striving to make the jury see the need to discredit the police's evidence and any conclusion the blood expert would arrive at, as their procedures were flawed.

While discussing the photos from the crime scene, David mentioned that there is a void area in the blood stain, which contains an oval shaped space having a different liquid substance. Evidence Technician Eric Campen maintained that none of the officers applied the chemical luminol on the wall bounding the stairway, as there was no apparent need because blood was completely visible on the walls.

"Does that show how luminol would look when it gets dry after application?" asked Rudolf, mentioning the strips on the wall. *"Yes, it does, to an extent. I can't tell what brought about those marks, but we didn't apply luminol on the walls, we never did,"* said Campen. *"Was it Michael trying to clean it before dialing 911 and then stopped midway?"*

Jim Hardin Jr, one of the prosecuting attorneys, surprisingly didn't bother to restore their witness's statement on redirect examination; instead, he allowed Campen to get off the stand, ignoring the points the defense raised during the thorough questioning.

In the absence of the jurors, David brought up an issue concerning a diagram that Campen had created using the computer, but deleted it later on, which had a set of possible footprints. The court had ordered that Campen provide the diagram, but it showed shoeprints and not footprints, and therefore was regarded as misleading. Judge Hudson reserved the decision to let the jury decide that the shortfall evidence weakened the prosecuting team's case, to the defense team's felicity.

Cause of Death Explained by a Medical Examiner

On August 6, 2003, the medical examiner, Dr. Kenneth Snell, who once concluded that Kathleen died from tripping on the steps, testified that he now had a different thought after he observed her wounds closely at the morgue. Dr. Snell, being a vital witness for the prosecutors, addressed the jury, saying that the seven lacerations he observed, as other forensic professionals conducted an autopsy on the victim's body, led him to believe that this was a case of a deadly beating and not an accident.

Though the police didn't find a likely

murder weapon, Kathleen's death was believed to be intentional, because of the amount and dispersion of the blood. Though a blood spatter professional would be testifying that the blood stains denoted the use of a tool, Dr. Snell said he was told, on the morning after the incident, by an evidence technician with the police who had some expertise in blood spatter, that Kathleen could have smashed her head on the steps of the staircase two or more times.

Dr. Snell said he observed two separate lesions which appeared as a tear on the victim's scalp, and as her hair was smeared with blood, he knew an autopsy was required, and he also asked the police to look for a crowbar or blow poke, believing only a tool or weapon with that shape could have brought about such lacerations, which could even be more at the back of her head that he couldn't see at the time.

Prosecutor Jim Hardin Jr. inquired why Snell now thinks it was intentional and not an accident. Dr. Snell replied that he initially made his conclusion outside of an autopsy.

"It's very common to alter the information in this field report as it was filed before the conduct of an autopsy," Snell said.

William Haggard, a forensic meteorologist who gave the analysis of weather conditions on the night of the incident, also gave his testimony before the jury. The prosecutors disputed that Peterson was smoking outside the house alone for 30 to 45 minutes while Kathleen fell and bled to death.

Haggard recited the weather conditions for that night -- it was about 53 degrees Fahrenheit in the early morning hours, and the permissible degree is about 70 degrees Fahrenheit for anyone to feel comfortable. Peterson was wearing a t-shirt and shorts while Kathleen was in a sweat suit.

The defense team practically made a mockery of Haggard's testimony. Haggard agreed he didn't know the basis of the tolerable degree, and he didn't inquire from anyone present in the house that night if they were comfortable with the temperature. Saying that Haggard made his deduction from readings provided by an airport located 30 miles away from the Peterson's house, Thomas Maher sought to discredit the witness's analysis.

"Is there now a weather station at the Peterson's house," asked Maher?

*****

Judge Hudson attended a hearing on whether to consider the emails and images taken from Michael's laptop. Though the counsel hadn't mentioned what the contents are, the court concluded that they were related to pornography.

In his opening remarks on July 1, 2003, Hardin told the jury that they had proof that Peterson's hard drive was formatted by someone after the death of the victim, who had loaded it with some other files. He told Judge Hudson he would get three professionals to prove it, depending on the judge's address of the admissibility question.

Witness Emphasized that Blood Marks are Pointing to the Accused

On August 14, 2003, according to the testimony given by a blood spatter analyst, small specks of blood, found on the wrong side of Peterson's shorts, implied that he must have been very close to the stairway when the incident occurred -- either based on a fall as claimed or based on a beating.

Later on, the jury would be listening to a testimony that was potentially detrimental to Peterson's case. The defense had propagated that 59-year-old Peterson was in the back of their house smoking when the incident happened to his spouse of five years.

North Carolina State Bureau Agent, Peter Duane Deaver, presented his conclusions to the judge in the absence of the jury so he could ascertain the soundness of the science. The judge later permitted the hearing of the testimony so the defense team could have a peek into Duane Deaver's deductions.

Deaver's conclusions include:

*   *Kathleen Peterson was attacked on the*

staircase by someone behind her, standing at the top of the stairs, who used a blunt tool. This finding was supported by the 'cast-off marks' present on the wall at the top stairway area.

*   *The deceased was struck repeatedly, and her head hit the steps several times, along with falling down.*

*   *Michael Peterson must have been close to the blood of Kathleen, in whatever position, when a heavy hit impacted his wife's head. This is due to the specks of blood on the back part of the wrong side of Peterson's shorts.*

*   *A little force creates large drops and big force creates little specks, Duane analyzed: "There is a tell-tale sign that someone left a blood trail in a failed attempt to remove the signs."*

*   *Two marks of blood on the steps seem to have occurred by a blow poke. The police couldn't locate any poke, but believed it was removed from the property by Peterson or anyone helping him. It would be similar to, or the one Kathleen's sister gave her family as a gift 15 years ago.*

David Rudolf unsuccessfully argued over the credibility of findings and forced the jury not to consider the evidence after cross-examining Deaver's report by asking some important questions.

Where was the Blow Poke? Jury Listened to the Facts Carefully

On September 4, 2003, Candace Zamperini, Kathleen's sister, who claimed to be very good with dates, recalled clearly gifting Kathleen a blow poke set during Christmas in 1984. She also recalled seeing and using the tool to light the fire at the Peterson's home the last time she traveled to North Carolina. *"It was on Thanksgiving Day in 1999, and it was just by the fireplace,"* she said on the witness stand.

Jim Hardin, the DA, presented an identical blow poke early in the trial and introduced it as an illustrative evidence, asking the jurors to feel the tool. David Rudolf's objection of the tool being passed to the jurors was disregarded. He said, *"It's not been offered as a real evidence."*

The District Attorney, as he steered the case to an end, showed Candace's photos from 1996 and 1998 which showed the missing tool in the family photographs. Peterson was expressionless as Candace spoke about her walking up the bloody stairs along with Michael and one of Kathleen's other sisters, after the police were done with their work at the scene.

Candace testified, *"Michael said, 'I ascended the staircase, I guess to get towels,' he looks back, and then down, and said, 'She fell all the way down the staircase."* The prosecuting counsel didn't express the importance of the statement. They would probably see it as Michael trying to drive home the idea that Kathleen's death was accidental.

Did the Performance of Prosecutors live up to their Expectations?

On September 6, 2003, were the prosecutors able to prove their case that Kathleen didn't fall, but was beaten to death by her husband, Michael?

Jim Hardin and Freda Black, the prosecutors, have now rested their case, and observers are ruminating over all the evidence, trying to figure out if they can produce proof beyond a reasonable doubt. Ten weeks have now passed; fifty witnesses have been presented by the prosecution, there have been photographs, documents, diagrams and other evidence, in the hundreds.

The defense team would be presenting witnesses who would express that Michael Peterson was crazy about Kathleen and that she was well treated and they never had a major fight that they knew of.

The prosecuting team had, however, discredited this portrayal when they presented the testimony of a male escort Michael had an online discussion with, where he tried to set up a meeting between them.

The state also presented an exhibit email in which Michael, or someone impersonating him, discussed the topic of homosexuality.

Judge Hudson's rulings, such as permitting the Ratliff case to be heard, is likely to help the defense's grounds for an appeal should Michael Peterson be convicted.

Defense's Case

Defense Discussed the Two-Fall Scenario in Kathleen's Death.

On September 9, 2003, a Neuropathologist, Dr. Jan Leetsma, took the stand to testify that Kathleen died as a result of slipping off the steep flight of stairs twice, at the base of which she was found lifeless.

"Due to excessive drinking, she might be tipsy and would have fallen down for the second time after successfully balancing herself at first."

A defense professional and author in Peterson's trial conclusively maintained that Kathleen's injuries, as a result of falling down the stairs, led to her death, not as purportedly stated that she was struck on the head repeatedly. He said this, even though it is in contradiction to some parts of his own book.

"There is not a contrecoup here," prosecuting counsel Jim Hardin stated, making reference to a section of the 1987 book written by Dr. Leetsma, where he explained the state of bruising caused by injuries to the brain. The book made it known that contrecoup, which occurs on the side opposite the area of the head that was hit, is a clear indication of falling on the back part of the head.

Dr. Jan Leetsma's testimony still gave credence to the theory that the deep cuts on

Kathleen's head, despite being abundant, could very will had been a result of a fall. Leetsma had spent a good period of the day being questioned by one of Peterson's attorneys.

The doctor declared that the lacerations, up to seven of them, which the prosecuting team stated were at the back of her head, are a misconception of the injuries. He explained to the jury that falling on even a flat surface could cause a complicated gash which might appear as though they are several smaller cuts in the scalp, but in fact are actually a result of a single large impact.

However, Dr. Deborah Radisch concluded the case for the prosecutors when she testified that the seven lesions found at the rear of Kathleen's head, coupled with the massive loss of blood, makes it a very clear case of manslaughter.

Dr. Leestma opposed Dr. Radisch's conclusions by drawing on the stained brain cell slides, diagrams of the skull and info from over 250 deaths caused by beatings in North Carolina, which were compiled by the office of the medical examiner.

"Kathleen's injuries occurred from a fall and not as a result of a deadly physical assault. I don't have any better explanation of my findings at the moment," Dr. Jan said.

Dr. Leestma expressed to the jury that

his conclusions are concrete and dependable and were substantiated with facts that Kathleen Peterson's injuries were:

1.   Inconsistent with the straight lesions that can be inflicted by a weapon that is cylindrical in shape – a blow poke from the fireplace being regarded as a possible murder weapon;

2.   Without a primary injury – which cancels out a possibility of a deadly beating – and

3.   Inconsistent with the deadly beating information collated by the examiner.

Jurors Heard Theory of Bloody Stairway Scene

On September 11, 2003, 18 steps, a narrow stairway base and a pool of blood: that's the picture members of the jury observed on a visit to the purported murder scene at the Peterson's home in Durham.

Demorris Lee, a reporter with the Raleigh News, was allowed to tag along with the jury. "*They were all involved and engrossed at the scene, taking notes and immersed in the surrounding of the staircase,*" he said.

The rear staircase at the Peterson's home, still in a bloody state, which connects the rooms on the second floor to the kitchen on the first floor, was the center of focus in Michael's murder case trial.

"They wondered how far they could ascend the steps of the stairway," the reporter said. *"A lot of them ascended up to four, five steps and turned to look, and also wave their hands, looking behind to see if they are likely to trip, or if they could get a grip on themselves without tripping."*

The opposition counsel believed 59-year-old Peterson struck his spouse of five years to her demise, and then proceeded to disguise it as a domestic mishap. Depending almost solely on tangible evidence, they took into account the seven lesions at the back part of the victim's head, the plenteous blood around the scene, and also the blood sprinkles, which all intimates she had been struck with an object.

The members of the jury were driven two miles from the court to the Peterson's home in two white vehicles. That availed them the opportunity to unravel conflicting reports personally, using enough pointers that could help in deciphering whether the scene was accurately being referred to as a crime scene, or just a place where an unpremeditated incident occurred.

Within the one hour spent at the Peterson's palatial home, the jurors surveyed the kitchen, the parlor, where Peterson was held by the police officials at their arrival to the house, and then the fireplace, from which the prosecuting attorneys implied he picked up a blow poke and used it to strike Kathleen to death.

David Rudolf, who asked the jurors to make the visit, believed the journey to the house was essential as photos which were presented to them in the courtroom couldn't sufficiently give them a true picture of the narrowness of the rearward flight of steps.

"It was necessary they see and assess the space themselves, to ascertain the possibility of the D.A.'s thoughts of what could have happened." David Rudolf narrated to reporters outside the home. *"It's a crucial move for us, so the members of the jury can see the difference between what they see in court, in pictures and videos, that it is different from what the space really looks like."*

An employee at David Rudolf's law firm read a section from the account of Christina Tomasetti, a friend to Todd, Peterson's son, who visited the Petersons on the night of the demise of Kathleen.

When Tomasetti was about to leave, at about 10.20 PM, she observed Michael opening a bottle of wine in the kitchen with the intention to watch a movie with Kathleen while they sipped on their glasses of wine.

She returned to the house at about 2.50 AM to witness a number of fire trucks and police cars all over the place.

"We discovered Mrs. Peterson had

tripped off the stairs and struck her head, thereby incurring a terrible head injury," said Tomasetti in her statement.

Defense Team Emphasized Over the Credibility of the Trial

There wasn't a perfect crime scene investigation on that fatal night; however, the one carried out by police officials at the Peterson's was rife with errors, testified a forensic analyst, Major Timothy Palmbach. When the defense lawyer questioned Palmbach, the Connecticut Division of Scientific Services' director, he used his forensic science experience and said:

"It's always a struggle and balance situation."

Mr. Palmbach, who earlier took the stand and later returned while the defense presented their case, said that the probity of a typical crime scene only comes after the duty of emergency responders to save lives, and even then, EMS officials should ensure the evidence is preserved.

When a person is pronounced dead, the Priority Area around the victim's body should be preserved, explained Palmbach. Any evidence should be packed up separately for protection's sake, so as to prevent the possibility of cross-contamination. The scene report should be documented in situ, and family members should also not be allowed to rush to touch the victim's body as Peterson and his son, Todd, did that night.

Some concerns raised by Palmbach were:

The victim's shoes were not packed separately; thus, cross-contamination could have taken effect.

Her glasses weren't picked up as evidence.

The towels at the scene weren't taken.

Sandals at the incident spot weren't taken.

More photos of the scene ought to have been appropriated, including very close shots of the blood splash evidence.

Considering his association with the State of Connecticut, Hardin questioned Palmbach regarding his partnership with Henry Lee to analyze evidence and forensic facts related to Peterson's trial.

The 11th Hour Surprise- What's Not There in the Fireplace?

September 23, 2003 – The most vital question needing an answer has always been, "Where can we find the murder weapon?" The prosecutors threw light over this fact and mentioned that a tool was missing from a stand in front of the fireplace that would have been used in Kathleen's murder.

Peterson's counsel brought forward an answer to the persistent question and produced a hollow, brass blow poke they purportedly found over the weekend, in good shape but dusty, in the Peterson's garage.

The sensational revelation of the blow poke created an interesting turn of events on the last day of Peterson's defense. His attorneys rested their case after nine witnesses in nine days declaring that Kathleen Peterson died when she fell down the stairway, accidentally, and not because of a deadly beating.

"*Did you ever bother to inquire from us if we found the blow poke?*" David Rudolf asked detective Art Holland, the lead police officer on the case.

"*No, I did not,*" he replied.

"*Did you then just presume it disappeared?*" asked Rudolf.

Holland answered after a pause, "*Disappeared or kept someplace?*"

Rudolf then drew out a cylindrical item wrapped in a plastic bag and moved towards the witness stand.

"*Can you see this?*" he asked the detective.

"*Yes, I can,*" said the detective.

"*It's a blow poke, isn't it?*" Rudolf said.

Though there wasn't a need to prove Peterson killed his wife with the blow poke, the item was made mention of so much in the case.

The opposing team who constantly flaunted the stand-in tool to buttress their case were slightly ruffled and focused on their notes as David Rudolf queried the witness.

Holland explained how he had intensively ransacked the Peterson's 10,000-square-foot abode for a likely tool or item that could have been used to effect the seven lesions on the back part of Kathleen's head. He also compared the two tools, observing that that of the defense was not of a similar size to the prosecutors' stand-in blow poke, that it was missing the pointy metal tip.

Detective Holland also discredited Rudolf's argument, which was that the blow poke was withheld from the defense team when they visited the property room. Judge Orlando Hudson Jr., without making it known to the prosecutors, instructed David Rudolf to let the investigators take the 'suspected murder weapon' into their custody.

Rebuttal Witness Claimed that Kathleen was Beaten to Death

Professor James McElhaney, on September 24, 2003, testified that Kathleen Peterson must have died after being beaten by a blunt object. The expert in injury biomechanics submitted to the jury of Michael Peterson's trial that a cylindrical light object must have been used to beat the victim to death, even if it was not necessarily a "blow poke" usually used for the fireplace.

According to the Duke University engineering professor, "*the kind of injuries the deceased sustained did not appear to have been from a fall but most likely from being beaten with a blunt round object.*" He supported the prosecution's theory that Michael Peterson must have killed his wife by mercilessly battering her in the stairwell of their mansion in North Carolina and then covering it up as an accident.

Peterson claimed to have been outside by the pool during the incident when his wife slipped and fell on the stairs. A missing blow poke from the fireplace suggested otherwise. His defense team, however, produced the "missing blow poke" in court, claiming to have found it in the garage and asserting that it showed no signs of having been used in the attack.

The defense had produced their own expert in injury biomechanics, Faris Bandak, who claimed that a close study of the injuries of the deceased pointed towards an accident. But

Professor McElhaney in contrast said that the number, location, orientation and length of the victim's injuries, combined with the energy amount and velocity that produced her head lacerations, couldn't have been from a fall.

The learned professor, however, added a "stretch" to his theory by admitting that there was a rare possibility of Kathleen Peterson's death to have resulted from an accident. She could have fallen against the stairs and doorway molding and sustained multiple injuries. The prosecutors nonetheless still pursued the blow poke theory as a most probable scenario.

Five months before Kathleen Peterson died, her younger sister Lori Hunt Campbell had paid her a visit along with sons Edward and William and her mother. This was July 2001, and Lori remembered how Edward kept playing with the blow poke by the fireplace. She said that her sister's house "*wasn't baby friendly*" and she had to warn baby Edward "*quit playing with the blow poke before you break something!*" Young Edward apparently "*delights in playing with guns, sticks and swords.*" If what they say is true, there was a missing poker. A missing murder weapon.

Prosecution Witness Perjured Himself

On September 26, 2003, Saami Shaibani found himself on the wrong side of the law, having lied to the court that he worked at Temple University. The judge ordered his testimony to be discarded after a letter from Temple's physics department chairman dated September 27, 2001, read:

"Mr. Shaibani was a constant fraudster who was not affiliated with the institution in any way."

The entire courtroom was thunderstruck by the revelation, and the prosecutor Jim Hardin Jr. firmly told Judge Orlando Hudson Jr. that *"the state would not be against the discarding of Shaibani's testimony if the court found him guilty of perjury."* The judge wasted no time and ruled that Shaibani had indeed perjured himself, instructing the jury to disregard his entire testimony.

Mr. Shaibani had testified that from his own perspective and tests he had done of falls on stairs, Kathleen Peterson's December 2001 death could not have resulted from such a fall. His lying could, however, land him in trouble because one could serve 10 to 20 months in jail under North Carolina law if found guilty of perjury.

"Do you understand, sir, that when you get on a witness stand and swear to tell the truth that it is perjury to lie even about something like what your position is at an university," Rudolf asked Shaibani.

"Yes, sir. I understand that," Shaibani

replied.

With the jury out of the courtroom, Rudolf insisted Shaibani's testimony be thrown out.

Shaibani came under heavy fire from the defense team who, apart from tearing up his credentials, dismissed his experimental tests as "silly" and "stupid." From having volunteers fall backwards on stairs to measure where they hit the doorjamb to "asking women to attempt to drown themselves by putting their heads in the toilet," Shaibani's ways were truly criticized as extreme.

Another Twist -- Pokers Reached from Two to Four!

It was a game of poker in the courthouse on September 29, 2003, where things shifted from people wondering about the "missing blow poke" to having a total of four blow pokes in the picture. The first in the list was a demonstration tool the prosecution had used to showcase the "blow poke theory". And then the defense produced the "found blow poke" said to have been in the garage.

Kathleen Peterson's sister, Candace Zamperini, had in 1986 gifted her siblings with matching blow pokes identical to the one she owned that was now used as the demonstration tool. She also brought two more pokes into the picture to make a total of four. The gifted ones totally matched the missing one, bringing up the conclusion that the missing poke had been found.

Another twist in the tale was when a similar staircase fall incident could have incriminated novelist Michael Peterson as a consistent mode of killing. This was Elizabeth Ratliff's death, whose daughters the novelist had adopted, and investigators ran tests to see if Margaret Ratliff was the biological daughter of Mr. Peterson. That would have given him the motive to kill her mother, but test results were negative.

Jurors now had a tough task ahead with several options on the table. They could use physical evidence like the spatter of blood found inside the khaki shorts of the novelist who still claims to have been by the pool when the incident happened. Detective Holland argued that:

"the missing poker couldn't have been in the garage because his team combed the 10,000-square-foot mansion thoroughly."

Tuesday would see jurors go through the entire evidence presented during the novelist's trial with the judge leading a charge conference where several issues like a probable second degree murder charge would be discussed.

After what had seemed like a lifelong trial that saw 65 witnesses take the stand and blow pokes totaling to four emerge on the scene, Michael Peterson's murder trial now seemed close to the end after three months of twists and turns in the courtroom. On Tuesday, September 30, 2003, a judge ordered deliberations by the jury to commence, signaling a looming end to the case. The final arguments would follow with the defense team.

*****

Michael Peterson had in 1985 been a neighbor to Elizabeth Ratliff in Germany when she was found dead below a staircase. The prosecution smelled a rat in Peterson's first degree murder trial in that his wife of five years, Kathleen Peterson, was also found dead in such a "staircase fall" incident. To them, this was not simply a mere coincidence.

Michael denied having been involved in the death of Elizabeth Ratliff, supporting his claim by the fact that he had raised her two children in good will after her demise. The two kids actually supported him during the trial, which emphasized his innocence.

The rules of evidence in North Carolina have an opening where prosecutors may use "*evidence from acts of the past*" to prove to the jury about possible "motive or intent of committing a crime and eliminating any possibility of the crime having been an accident." This opening gave the prosecution a window to open up Elizabeth Ratliff's death in Germany. How Judge Orlando Hudson would address this evidence was a contentious issue among the lawyers.

Upon further investigation by the investigation team, they came to learn about another death of a woman who was also linked with Michael Peterson. Not only was Kathleen found dead on the staircase, but one of their neighbors from his previous residence died in the same way.

While he was living with Patricia Peterson, his first wife, and two sons, Todd and Clayton, Elizabeth Ratliff was among their good and close friends. Patricia, aka Patty, and Elizabeth were friends when they both used to teach in a German school. Then she married Michael, who later on went to serve his state in the Vietnam War. Patty moved to the Rhein-Main Airbase situated near Frankfurt and continued her services as a second-grade teacher.

After spending his tenure in Vietnam, Michael retired as Captain and came back to his family in Germany, where they befriended Elizabeth and her husband, George Ratliff, who was also a Captain in the Army. Both families used to spend a good deal of time in each other's company and, therefore, their bond was famous among the neighborhood. Michael and Patricia became parents of two sons, Todd and Clayton, while George and Elizabeth gave birth to two daughters, Martha and Margaret.

None of them were aware of what was coming next to them. Elizabeth and George were unaware of how their lives were going to change. In 1983, tragedy struck the family when George was killed in a military operation. Elizabeth was shocked by the news while frightened at the same time about how she would be able to raise their two daughters alone! That was the time when she began to rely upon Michael and Patricia more than anyone. They used to eat together, and Michael even helped Elizabeth take care of her daughters.

But, just like before, everything changed once again, and the Ratliff family had to face another trauma as Elizabeth was found dead on the stairs of her home in Grafenhausen, Germany. There were claims that Michael was the last person who saw Elizabeth before she died and, therefore, he was suspected for her murder as well.

The 43-year-old mother of two daughters died on November 27, 1985, when her children's nanny, Barbara Malagnino, found her lying at the bottom of the staircase. As soon as she saw the body, she immediately called Patricia Peterson, her neighbor, for help. She then called the police, and both ladies gave their statements of what they had seen in the home. According to Barbara:

"Everything was in place, except that Elizabeth was lying on the staircase with no signs of life. However, there was not that much blood around her."

Soon after the German police started their investigation, they declared Elizabeth's death an accident. When her death case was mentioned during Michael's trial for the murder of his second wife, Kathleen Peterson, the prosecutor called Patricia as the prime witness. She said:

"I was sitting here directly observing when the German medical examiner took a spinal tap and held up the contents so that he could view [it]" said Patty. *"Even from this distance I could see that it did not look clear, and that's when he made the statement, right there by her body in my presence, that she had died of a cerebral hemorrhage."*

Michael and Patricia took the responsibility of the two orphaned girls, Margaret and Martha, with an intention to provide them with as normal a life as their parents would have given them. The family lived a normal life until the couple, Michael and Patricia, decided to separate the following year. Michael, along with Margaret and Martha, moved to the U.S. Patricia remained in their Durham home with her two sons, Todd and Clayton.

The Exhumation

During the retrial hearing of Kathleen's murder (which was nowhere near to being an accident in my opinion), the police department got their prime suspect, Michael, who was the last person to see Kathleen, considering the deviations between what he said about the incident and what they had actually found.

As soon as the prosecution looked into the death of Elizabeth and noticed the coincidence between the two cases, Kathleen's death took another twist, and this time, the investigation went down to another retrial! Since she also fell down the stairs and the German police declared it an accident without giving much attention to investigation, the Superior Court ordered the police department to exhume Elizabeth's body from her grave in Texas so that her injuries could be reassessed in order to be certain about the actual cause of her death. The court's major intention was to ensure that whatever had been assumed for 17 years was either true or there was something that still needed attention.

Permission was taken from Elizabeth's sister and mother, and the authorities acted as per orders and made arrangements for the exhumation. Michael was quite upset at the court's decision to exhume Elizabeth's body for re-examination.

Following the court's instructions, the state medical examiner carried out a second autopsy on April 16, 2003. Although David Rudolf, Michael's lawyer, requested to appoint a 'neutral' pathologist' for Elizabeth's autopsy, ignoring his request, the District Attorney appointed Dr. Deborah L. Radisch for the job since she was the state pathologist.

Her reports concluded that the injuries on Elizabeth Ratliff's head were due to a homicidal assault -- contrary to what was reported on her death certificate. The facts were pointing towards Michael's involvement in her death as well since he was the last person who had seen Elizabeth before her so-called 'fall'. To defend his client, David Rudolf claimed that the wordings used in the reports were quite inflammatory and wrong with respect to what should be present in the autopsy. Comparing Deborah's autopsy with 260 autopsies from blunt trauma, he made a lot of objections on her credibility. For him, the claim of multiple force impacts was blunt and misleading.

According to Deborah's autopsy, there were seven deep lacerations, similar to Kathleen's, on Elizabeth's head which were caused due to blunt force trauma. The state pathologist explained that the actual injuries were quite different from what victims usually had when they fell down a few stairs. Instead, they are the clear sign of multiple force impacts. She shared her views that these injuries were caused when she was alive.

This report by the pathologist was submitted to the Superior Court as supporting evidence for the prosecution to strengthen their claims that Michael was the murderer.

Everyone present in Elizabeth's aftermath was called to give statements, while the state pathologist was brought to the witness stand to tell of her analysis on Mrs. Ratliff's injuries and those similarities with Kathleen's death.

Here, the considering aspect is that Elizabeth's death facts wouldn't have much impact over the jury because the case was quite old, but Michael's conviction in Kathleen's murder in October 2003 should be easy to figure out. The decision turned out to be unanimous by the jury.

Upon seeing the evidence against their guardian, Martha and Margaret, daughters of Elizabeth Ratliff, still stood by Michael and showed their complete support to him. They believed that their mother's death was an accident and, for them, Michael was innocent.

So the conclusion of Elizabeth Ratliff was still confusing as there was no clear evidence of Michael's involvement in her death. Though some people believe that the two were having an illicit relationship, this was strenuously denied by his first wife, Patricia Peterson.

Defense Team Raises 10 Reasons Why Michael Peterson Wouldn't Have Killed Kathleen

David Rudolf is an accomplished attorney who represented the troubled novelist fully. On Thursday, October 2, 2003, he presented a Top 10 list of why Michael wouldn't have killed Kathleen.

First, there was no longer a missing murder item because the suspected blow poke had been found and showed no evidence of having been used in the said attack.

Second, there was no clear intent why Michael Peterson would have any reason to hurt Kathleen. There was just no motive.

Third, he argued that a close couple, without any previous instances of hostility, could just not have initiated violence with a brutal murder.

Fourth, all court attendees would agree that the emotions and grief portrayed by Peterson throughout the trial all came out of sincerity and genuinely from the heart.

Fifth, a beating leading to death would cause brain bruising from trauma and fractures to the skull and other parts of the body. Therefore, Kathleen Peterson definitely did not die from a beating as no such injuries were found on the victim at autopsy.

Sixth, focused on the bloodstain evidence which showed not to have any resemblance to a beating incident due to the following reasons:

a. The fact that no castoff was visible on ceilings and walls certainly disobeyed physics laws.

b. The wall had spatter on it which, upon analysis, would not have resulted from Kathleen Peterson's head getting smashed.

c. The quantity of spatter on the walls made it impossible for Kathleen Peterson's death to have resulted from a beating because the suspect's sneakers and socks would have had more blood than was found.

d. If Michael Peterson had indeed committed the murder, his glasses and watch would have sustained a substantial amount of spatter relative to the amount witnessed on the walls, which was not the case.

e. If indeed a beating had occurred during that fateful day, the suspect Michael Peterson would most likely have gotten spatter on the front of his shorts rather than on his backside where blood was found.

f. The theory of dilution that the state presented was totally senseless.

g. The victim's pants tested positive for a shoe print, but it faced away from her body.

h. The empty area was not a clean-up

but a "shadow" as Dr. Lee had explained.

Seventh, purported documentation and information from the crime scene were unreliable. It was garbage coming in and garbage going out.

Eighth, whereas science relies on true facts, the state in Michael Peterson's first degree murder trial seemed to ignore real science restrictions and seemed to lean more towards junk science.

Ninth, the state seemed to have been led by guesswork and emotion throughout Peterson's murder trial.

Tenth, to conclude the magical list, defense attorney Rudolf likened the investigation by the state to "tunnel vision," asking for an indictment before presenting sufficient evidence.

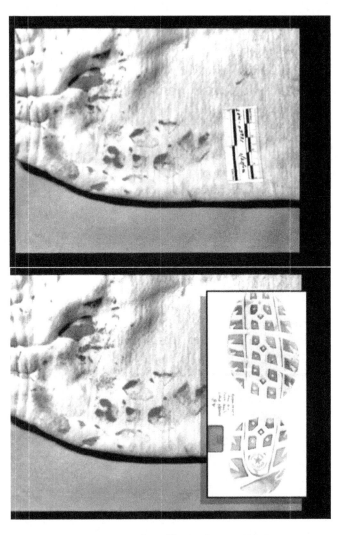

Source: Forensic Files, S11, E22
A Novel Idea, 13:39

*****

October 3, 2003, saw the prosecutors

presenting their closing argument. They argued that although the deceased could not personally testify in the case, the circumstances surrounding her death, and the evidence found at the murder scene was enough to convict the novelist.

Prosecutor Jim Hardin staged an emotional closing argument referring to a photograph from the stairwell where the late Kathleen Peterson had met her fate. Pointing to the blood-spattered walls, the legal expert submitted that "*from the red-stained walls, the victim is screaming out loud for justice to be served and the truth established.*"

Mr. Hardin further advised the court that the case was a simple matter of common sense, addressing the kind of injuries the victim had sustained as well as the blood spatter found at the murder scene. He said, "*even if one was to fall down stairs, there was no practically possible way that one would sustain 38 injuries over their back, face, head, wrists and hands even if the victim underwent two falls. In Kathleen's case, the stairs fall theory is absolutely senseless.*"

Having taken the mantle from fellow counterpart Freda Black on submission of the final argument by the state, prosecutor Jim Hardin clearly expressed to the jury that Michael Peterson's alibi on the day of Kathleen's death was a lie. He stated that "*by following one's intuition, it's very clear that something does not add up in Michael Peterson's version of the story."*

Prosecutor Freda Black reminded the court that they were dealing with a renowned novelist, Michael Peterson, to whom the case was just another story of fiction in the making. The prosecution maintained that the 59-year-old had not been by the pool as claimed but instead had clobbered his wife using a rounded blunt object. The recovery of the missing blow poke in the basement garage of his North Carolina mansion also raised eyebrows as the item had gone missing from the house in mysterious circumstances.

The Jury Deliberates

On October 6, 2003, the case was turned over to the jury to determine whether Michael Peterson indeed killed his wife or lost her to a staircase fall accident. The jury was comprised of seven women, three of whom were nurses, and five men.

A "drunk and disorderly" juror who had been detained the previous evening for inappropriate behavior lost his seat in the panel to a 37-year-old female alternate juror. The manager at an institute of clinical research and mother of two children was elected as the foreperson of the jury.

Judge Hudson dismissed Wilford Elis Hamm, a former carpenter, from the jury panel and assured jurors all records of proceedings would be sealed. Another juror, Joanne Rebecca Hairston, was shown the door when it emerged that she mocked the accused who was a customer at the bank where she was employed.

During the first few days, the jurors requested several pieces of evidence in their deliberation sessions which were brought in by the court clerks. Some of the evidence items requested were the four blow pokes that had largely dominated Peterson's murder trial, blood-spattered shoes, and a "boom box" that could play Michael's call to 911 for the jury.

Thursday October 8, 2003, saw the day end on a usual note with Judge Orlando Hudson warning jurors to be wary of any media exposure on the case until it was closed. However, the ever-preying media hawks never sleep, and one juror produced an invitation letter from a local TV station to discuss the case live after a verdict had been reached. Sonya Pfeiffer, a local reporter, had sent the letter to the juror stating, "*your thoughts on the case would be much appreciated as the evidence phase has already passed.*"

In an ongoing case, the media should not engage active jurors until they have completed the deliberations stage. Any such act can hold such media houses or individuals in contempt, as was the case with Philadelphia Magazine staff writer Carol Saline in 2002, when she engaged a juror in the murder trial of Rabbi Fred Neulander.

The jurors also cross checked testimonies from two key witnesses: North Carolina chief medical examiner John Butts, and Duke University engineering professor James McElhaney. Butt asserted that since only a microscopic amount of blood had been found in Kathleen's lungs, it was not possible that she could have coughed up blood to stain the stairwell as insinuated by the defense. Dr. McElhaney, an expert in the field of injury biomechanics, also ruled out any possibility of the victim's head wounds having resulted from a staircase fall.

Judge Orlando Hudson cautioned the jurors to keep their "eyes" and "ears" open, jokingly stating that "*having 12 jurors in total was for, among other reasons, so that the courtroom would have 24 ears and 24 eyes at all times.*"

The Verdict

It only took the jury a few days to reach its decision. It was a memorable day on Friday, October 10, 2003, when the moment everyone had been waiting for arrived.

No one heard the knock Friday except Sheriff's Deputy Bryan Mister. He opened the deliberation room door, listened for an instant, then closed it. He turned to the dozens of people keeping vigil in Courtroom No. 1 and said, "*We have a verdict.*"

Peterson took his seat between his attorneys. His family huddled in the gallery. Superior Court Judge Orlando Hudson brought in the jury, and the forewoman produced a manila envelope. Mister delivered it to Hudson, who handed it to court clerk, Angela Kelly. She withdrew a sheet of paper and read it.

"State of North Carolina versus Michael Iver Peterson, File No. 01 CRS 24821: We the 12 members of the jury unanimously find the defendant to be guilty of first-degree murder, this the 10th day of October 2003."

The blood drained from Mike Peterson's face and, for a moment, he did not move.

The jury convicted Peterson of battering his late wife Kathleen to death in their North Carolina home. Emotions ran high in the courtroom with the occasional click and clack of cameras from the photographers hungrily taping the moment and running for the doors to report the breaking news.

Elizabeth Ratliff's two daughters who had been raised by Peterson seemed most affected by the proceedings. When the verdict was read aloud by the court clerk, Martha and Margaret Ratliff cried quietly and were only calmed down by Peterson's sons, Todd and Clayton. Their father struggled to keep his composure, and upon getting a last chance to speak from Judge Orlando Hudson before his sentencing, told his children that "*It's OK.*" That was so much calm from a man who was about to spend the rest of his life in prison without any possibility of parole.

Michael Peterson's defense attorney David Rudolf had put up a spirited fight during the trial and stated that he would certainly file an appeal against the ruling. He watched sadly as his client left the courtroom in handcuffs to a lifetime in prison. The Ratliffs sobbed, watching their 'dad' being taken away, and even Michael's reassurance that "*It's all right*" didn't seem to calm them down.

Having been a newspaper columnist at one point, Michael Peterson had received a lot of support from the surrounding community throughout his trial. This made prosecutors decide to not pursue a death penalty against him.

During his trial, Michael Peterson had been free on bail of $850,000, but after the verdict, that freedom ended. Although having announced that he would file an appeal, defense lawyer David Rudolf did not request a bond hearing. The three-month trial had been a rigorous one with over 800 items of evidence analyzed and 65 witnesses taking the stand. One juror admitted that "*the beginning of deliberations was not a smooth phase as the direction kept shifting and several votes had to be taken to sort it out.*"

Prosecutor Freda Black, however, empathized with the Peterson and Ratliff families although she felt that justice had been served in the case. The prosecution had successfully convinced the jury to overlook Michael Peterson's "fictional plan" of covering up the murder as an accident. The novelist's close family, however, had a tough moment on their hands with Freda Black noting that,

"[M]y heart goes out to the Peterson and Ratliff families for they harbor genuine feelings for Mr. Peterson and it will be a very difficult day witnessing his sentencing."

The Owl or the Husband: Who's the Real Culprit?

Back in 2009, another theory related to Kathleen's death emerged when T. Lawrence Pollard, a Durham attorney and a neighbor of the Petersons, proposed that an owl could be the reason for Kathleen's death as she ran to protect herself from its attack and ended up falling down the stairs, causing her head to hit the treads of the steps.

Although he wasn't directly involved in the case, he had been following its public proceedings, and after carefully examining the findings and words from witnesses, he took a step ahead and gave his approach towards Kathleen's death.

After analyzing the evidence from the State Bureau of Investigation (SBI) in North Carolina, he suggested that 'the feather,' as mentioned in the evidence list, could be the turning point for the case. Later on, the defense team determined that the SBI lab report mentioned a wooden sliver from a tree limb and an owl feather clutched in the victim's left hand while she was struggling to protect herself from the object.

After Lawrence Pollard completed his owl theory, District Attorney Jim Hardin and Freda Black, his assistant, pooh-poohed the idea by mentioning state pathologist Deborah

Radisch's lab report in which she didn't testify about the owl feather. Rather, she claimed that the wounds on Kathleen Peterson's head would have been caused by a 'blow poke.' Once the prosecution was finished with their arguments, Michael's lawyer David Rudolf sprang into action and, taking a bold step to prevent his failure, forced the court to cross-examine Deborah's report once again. He supported his request by saying that an aluminum hollow tube with a sharp blade couldn't kill Kathleen in the way she was found. He called Deborah into the witness stand and asked, is it possible to have hematomas or contusions from the blow poke on the head? Based upon her experience, she said "No." Then he further asked, how could a blow poke kill Kathleen? She didn't have the answer to this question as well.

Radisch seemed to be quite speechless to whatever David was saying as she was not in a position to explain how Michael could kill his wife with a blow poke, especially when it comes to having hollow wounds on her head. When this owl theory was introduced, there was quite a lot of evidence to prove that owls are known to attack people and cause severe injuries. There was an incident reported in which a man was attacked by an owl when he was leaving his workplace. The whole incident was captured by the security cameras. Pollard also brought him into his press conference when he was discussing the owl theory involved in Kathleen's case. A victim, a young boy, mentioned that the owl knocked him down and caused severe bleeding from his head.

Press Release
Thursday, August 21, 2008
Judicial Building
Durham, North Carolina

POTENTIAL EXONERATING EVIDENCE FOUND IN PETERSON MURDER CASE

Member of the Press. We are here today to announce significant news in the Michael Peterson murder case of 2001. Mr. Peterson was convicted in 2003 of murdering his wife, Kathleen. Shortly after the conviction, a new theory arose as to what might have happened to Mrs. Peterson – i.e., The Owl Theory. The D.A.'s office dismissed it as absurd, citing the absence of feathers, and most people labeled it ridiculous. Always the same question was asked by the authorities and press – Where are the feathers? Well, folks, we are here today announcing that the feather has been found. And what's more important is where the feather was found – entwined in the hair of Kathleen Peterson that was pulled out by the root ball and clutched in her left hand! This is the most significant clue found yet in this mysterious murder case because it comes from ground zero on that fateful December night in 2001, and it points us directly to Kathleen's attacker. The microscopic feather is the equivalent of a nuclear piece of exculpatory and/or exonerating evidence and must be immediately examined forensically to find its origin. It clearly shows that something avian was on Mrs. Peterson's head at the time of the assault. Because owls have tiny microscopic feathers that cover their legs, feet, and toes all the way to the talons, and because owls are primarily nocturnal, this may be from one, transferred to Mrs. Peterson's hair.

The feather was discovered by a member of Peterson's defense team as she was going back through the old files and boxes of documents in this case. A routine examination of an SBI crime lab report on fiber and hair analysis done on February 19, 2002 (over six years ago), yielded this amazing discovery. It is truly a remarkable job of research, and we all owe her a great debt of gratitude for her diligence and sharp acumen in finding it. We are confident it will ultimately lead to Mr. Peterson being proven an innocent man.

The importance of the feather cannot be overstated, because (1) it comes from the wounds on top of Mrs. Peterson's head, and (2) it is the equivalent of not just DNA of the attacker in Mrs. Peterson's hand, but a whole body part (albeit a small one). Rest assured, if this feather had been a hair from Michael Peterson, rather than a feather, the State would have been waiving it in front of the jury like a red flag in front of a bull! The fact that it is a feather instead of Michael Peterson's hair or DNA makes it no less significant.

Therefore, the defense team of Michael Peterson is formally requesting the District Attorney's office to officially reopen the investigation of Mrs. Peterson's death and immediately photograph, test, and analyze this overlooked and newly discovered evidence. Inasmuch as the feather has been in the possession of the State of NC for almost 6 years and because the State denied its existence and has repeatedly [been] asked for the feathers, we respectfully submit that it is the State's responsibility, and moral obligation, to do this immediately. We say this because it is the duty of the D.A.'s office to seek justice and follow any and all potentially exonerating evidence and not just seek a conviction. If the feather is proven to be from a raptor or any avian creature that could inflict these types of injuries, then Mr. Peterson should be immediately exonerated and released from custody.

Indeed, this feather can prove Mr. Peterson an innocent man and provide for his freedom immediately.

T. Lawrence Pollard
Attorney at Law
128 E. Parrish Street
Durham, NC 27701

So it can be said that the owl theory was actually more valid than the blow-poke idea! This 'invisible' weapon was presented by the prosecution when Kathleen's sister, Candace Zamperini, mentioned that she gifted her one which was missing from the crime scene. In the beginning, nobody was convinced by the owl theory as it made no sense to anyone but, after some time, it was realized that the theory was discredited purposefully.

While most of the people were not convinced by the owl theory, there were still some from the media who took his facts seriously and asked him how could an owl enter the Peterson's mansion. Instead of claiming that an owl found a place to get into the home, Pollard stated that Kathleen was attacked in the yard, which led to the next important question: So where were the feathers then? To be honest, the answer was quite obvious: the police never looked for feathers outside the crime scene.

Some critics also asked: Where is the blood then? If an owl attacked Kathleen outside the home, why didn't the place have any blood marks? Yes, no one was interested enough to look for it, but still, the initial report mentioned blood stains on the door and porch from where she re-entered the home. The next question arising out of the discussion was: how could she die from an owl's attack and how did blood stains spread on the staircase?

Pollard cleared this confusion by giving the statement that when an owl attacked Kathleen and she ran inside to protect herself, her blood was all the way across the floor that led to creating her footprints in blood on the staircase.

Durham Attorney Declined the Request to Reopen the Case

Durham Attorney T. Lawrence Pollard filed three affidavits to the Superior Court about reopening the case because he found compelling evidence of Michael being innocent in Kathleen Peterson's death in 2001 and he refused to accept the guilty charge.

However, new progress in the discovery mentioned the presence of more feathers in the victim's left hand. He further explained that these findings should have materially affected the jury's deliberation and final verdict. The victim might have lost more microscopic feathers, but still, some traces were left in her hand.

The next argument by the attorney brought a new twist to Michael's trial as the defense was not aware of a tire iron from the neighborhood. Prosecution responded by saying that it had nothing to do with Kathleen's murder and, therefore, the judge refused to consider his request.

The request somehow managed to

receive coverage by the media, and some of the representatives started to question the manner of investigation by the State Bureau of North Carolina. Michael's children also sent a letter to the News & Observer stating that these evidences should be considered and their father must have a new trial.

Pollard suggested Hudson hold off his decision until the defense lawyers discuss and complete paperwork. He shared his views as:

"We still have some hope. Although the incident happened late at night, we got the feather. We also know that a small wooden slither [sic] was also recovered from the victim's hand, which was found to have been related to a tree limb. Sadly, the SBI lab agents didn't pay attention to the feathers. They shouldn't think that they had nothing to do with the case!"

While talking about the affidavits, it's important to look into the fact that they included a letter from the genetics program of Robert C. Fleischer of the Smithsonian National Museum of Natural History. He mentioned that he wanted to do DNA test of the feathers in order to find out the species of bird.

Dr. Alan van Norman, one of the lab agents, explained that there was a pair of two lacerations on the victim's scalp, each having a trident appearance, with three limbs joining at 30 degrees from each other while a fourth limb converges at 180-degree from the center limb.

According to the affidavit, Norman is a retired US Army surgeon who was employed to work as an owl expert and neurosurgeon in North Dakota. He mentioned that, after a brief examination, Kathleen's injuries were not consistent with respect to what a blunt object could cause; rather, these injuries were quite consistent with a large bird attack.

Dr. Patrick T. Redig also agreed to Pollard's theory in his study at the University of Minnesota. He was the person behind the second affidavit in which, he said:

"According to my professional exposure, the acclaimed attack at the back and face of victim's head was quite obviously from a large owl. It could be expected to see such lacerations and punctures."

While writing the third affidavit, Kate P. Davis, Raptors of the Rockies' executive director, agreed with the hypothesis and explained that it would be possible for owls to show such behavior and kill humans like this.

"The lacerations present on the victim's scalp are quite similar to those created by a raptor's talons. Possibilities are high that she might have resisted the attack from the back of the head due to which, there were feathers in her hand. The configuration and size also indicate that the attack would have been done by a Barred owl."

Deaver Convinced Jurors About Michael's Conviction

During Michael Peterson's trial, Duane Deaver, blood-spatter expert, gave his testimony in which he explained that the blood present on the staircase wall and on Michael's clothes was evidence that the accused was guilty of the first-degree murder of Kathleen Peterson. His testimony played a crucial role in sending Michael behind bars. His perjured testimony played a decisive role in Peterson being released.

He testified before, but after many requests and a struggle to convince jurors to hear the testimony, Deaver finally managed to bring his analysis in front of the court. Four men and eight women showed interest in his testimony. In the beginning of his explanation, he said:

"The forceful impact started from step 16 whose pressure was entirely on the surface. The head of the victim was hit with so much force that it was not possible to have happened from a fall."

Jim Hardin was the person behind Deaver's explanation of the blood-spatter analysis. With the help of a silver model and photographs of the back staircase, he presented the results of his experiments with bloody clothes, mannequin heads and sponges.

Some jurors took a closer look at his poster boards and diagrams since it could be a turning point for prosecution as the testimony declared Michael as a murderer. The 18-year veteran from the SBI explained to the jury that the victim was hit three times at the back of her head with a hard object which caused her to fall off the stairs immediately. Upon analysis of the blood spatters on Michael's shoes and shorts, he predicted that he was standing right behind Kathleen when she died. He supported his argument by showing Converse sneakers and said:

"The bloodstains on the shoes are the result of forceful impact, but I couldn't tell the height from where they are created."

Hardin, with the help of state's exhibit 72, questioned whether Deaver had seen something like that before. He replied that such blood marks could have been caused by the fireplace tool, i.e., the blow poke. There were similar bloodstains on Kathleen's left leg. As with the evidence, he showed the pictures of his experiment in which he pressed the end of the tool against the poster board and a bloody paper towel. Both had the same marks.

Another confusing part was the absence of the fireplace tool when Deaver searched the crime scene on December 9, 2001. Surprisingly, he found everything perfectly in order during his second visit on June 27, 2002, when the fireplace set was the same as new.

At the end of the hearing, Hardin asked Deaver if he had a conclusion about what exactly had happened with Kathleen that night. Using his silver pointer, he explained the entire testimony that the attacker, outside the stairwell, had used a hard object to hit victim's head. Facing down the stairs, she struck her head thrice, and there was blood everywhere after a few seconds.

"There must be bloodstains on step 17 as well. But I believe that they were cleaned purposely when Kathleen was lying on step 18," he added.

Upon hearing Deaver's blood testimony and analysis, the jurors were more certain about Michael's conviction.

Tim Palmbach, who was the departmental chairman at the University of New Haven, pointed out some valid objections in Peterson's murder trial. When he was arrested on December 9, 2001, for his wife's murder, Duane Deaver proposed blood testimony that led Michael to his guilty verdict and life imprisonment.

He made many requests to reconsider testimony throughout his sentence but wasn't successful. Palmbach, as one of the defense witnesses in the trial, claimed that Deaver's theory to identify the source of bloodstains on the staircase was misleading and it was full of flaws. He stated that Deaver focused on a few blood droplets and didn't mention to the jurors that there were some bloodstains he never tested.

When the State Bureau of Investigation became aware that Duane Deaver had submitted a false report in 2003 and committed perjury in Michael's trial, Peterson received approval for a retrial, thus receiving another chance to prove his innocence. Deaver was fired in 2011 after which time more cases were proved to have been falsified. Deaver was shown to falsify up to 34 previous criminal cases as reported by the authorities.

One such case was related to Kirk Turner, whom Deaver wrongfully testified against and was paramount in his conviction for his wife's murder in 2007. When Turner's innocence was proven, he sued Deaver and his fellow SBI agent for $200,000, which was settled in 2018. Kirk claimed that the agents filmed the entire scene on their own, keeping in mind that the results should match. As the result of their compromise over duties, Kirk was also awarded $4.25 million as a settlement from the State of North Carolina.

Retrial Hearing

Michael Peterson's counsel in the retrial submission stated that the captious column written by Peterson for Herald-Sun, a Durham newspaper, from years 1997 to 1999, infuriated the Police Department and County District Attorney's Office of Durham and also influenced their rather abrupt decision to investigate him.

"The approach employed by the Durham Police and the N.C Bureau of Investigation in the probe of Kathleen Peterson's death, coupled with the District Attorney's hasty move to charge Michael Peterson, strongly implied an earnest resolve to indict Mike for the demise of his spouse," stated the submission.

According to the submission, the State embraced an open-file transparency statute which mandates that, after investigation, law enforcement release all evidence, notes and test results to the defense prior to the retrial.

"If any communications were made within the police of Durham or another enforcement team, whether it's in written form or not, demonstrating extreme dislike or partiality against Michael Peterson because he criticized the enforcement of the law personnel, it isn't likely the Durham Police would divulge that information during the 2003 initial trial. Although, now, the open-file policy of North

Carolina now mandates that such communication be disclosed in accordance with the new governing statutes."

President of Bevel, Gardner & Associates, an Oklahoma-based forensic science consulting company, Thomas Bevel, hinted that Deaver, whom the SBI had relieved of his duties, hadn't improved himself professionally by taking training courses in more than 20 years and did not belong to any professional organizations. Consequently, he didn't have any peer review which might have improved his work in some way.

Bevel went on further in his testimony to say that Deaver's handling of Michael's case was below standard and lacked professionalism, and he didn't document his findings about the blood found at the base of the stairway appropriately.

Bevel got a bit dramatic in the court room when he hit the wall with his head, with the intention of explaining to the court the possibility of Kathleen injuring herself accidentally as opposed to being murdered.

Tracey Cline, a District Attorney in Durham, opposed Bevel's thoughts, arguing that he hasn't reviewed evidence from the trial.

She went further to ask Bevel to say categorically if, in his opinion, Deaver was right or wrong. Bevel, however, answering indirectly said, *"There are too many gray areas in this case that I do not agree with."*

An investigator from Charlotte, Ronald Guerette said, after he thoroughly scrutinized Deaver's files at the State Bureau of Investigation, he observed that he hadn't been at a crime scene for more than four years before handling Peterson's case.

Tracey Cline, on the other hand, proceeded to prove that Deaver's testimony was correct. She firmly believed Peterson should be denied a retrial.

Tom Metzloff, a law professor at Duke University, who closely observed the first trial back in 2003, said one cannot make sudden plays as with a standard football match. The retrial would be different as the opposition team is very aware and ready.

"Some of those superficial matters like the sexuality concern of Michael being bi-sexual, and the neighbor's death in Germany, wouldn't come in anymore as testimony," he further said.

As a reference, the North Carolina Supreme Court in 2007 ruled against the search which led to the finding of emails exchanged between Peterson and a male escort, saying the finding was very insufficient, as the investigators were unable to put forward a good reason to go through Michael's personal computers.

The prosecuting attorneys were bent on

the hunch that the emails and evidence from the male escort implied that the Petersons were having troubles in their marriage, and so that could very well be a probable motive for the murder of Kathleen by her husband, Michael.

The Court did conclude that rendering the search null and void wouldn't suffice to have reversed Michael's conviction at that time. It would, however, exclude introduction in a fresh trial, that is, all the proof concerning the escort and any other testimony retrieved from Mike's personal computers.

Peterson mentioned during an interview years ago that he felt bad not being able to testify in his own defense, which meant he was likely to take to the witness stand himself during the retrial.

As there would be different testimonials in the retrial, so also would there be a different set of people.

Judge Jim Hardin, a former Durham District Attorney, and Freda Black, an assistant prosecuting counsel, were lawyers in private practice. Tracy Cline said she would request that the North Carolina Attorney General's Office execute the prosecution.

Hudson presided over the initial trial. He revealed he would be asking the administrative office of North Carolina to assign a different judge to oversee the retrial. Rudolf also mentioned not being certain he would be continuing as Peterson's defense counsel.

In his 39-pages ruling, Hudson, the presiding judge in the Peterson case, wrote that Duane Deaver confused both the jurors and himself about his competence and the correctness of his blood tests. The judge went further in his write-up to say that he would never have permitted Deaver to stand as a witness if he had known Duane puffed his abilities, and even other experts in blood spatter doubted his tests.

"Duane's evidence steered the consultations and the jurors' verdict in the wrong direction," Hudson wrote. *"Duane's misstatements and the acceptance of his methods and findings had a huge impact on the proceedings of Peterson's trial."*

Hudson ruled that prosecuting counsel were required to put Peterson's attorneys in the know of Duane's favoritism and questionable scientific methods of tests he conducted prior to the 2003 trial. Failure to make this notification equates to the violation of a fair hearing for Peterson.

*****

On November 14, 2016, Michael Peterson's petition for the evasion of a retrial was denied. A fresh trial was thereby slated for March 8, 2017. But about this time, a resolution was being negotiated by Rudolf –

representing Peterson again – and the DA of Durham County.

Peterson accepts an Alford Plea

After realizing that the SBI agent had provided misleading evidence, the court allowed retrial of his wife Kathleen's murder case in order to make sure that he could use all the methods available to prove his innocence.

But on February 24, 2017, Peterson accepted an Alford Plea -- (*An Alford Plea is a guilty plea of a defendant who proclaims he is innocent of the crime, but admits that the prosecution has enough evidence to prove that he is guilty beyond a reasonable doubt. It is entered when an accused, together with his attorney, has made the calculated decision to plead guilty because the evidence against him is so strong that it will likely lead to conviction. Typically, it results in a guilty plea of a lesser crime (i.e., second degree murder rather than first degree). Some states see the Alford Plea invoked frequently, such as Louisiana, Michigan, Missouri, Pennsylvania and Ohio; however, the United States Military, along with Indiana and New Jersey, forbid its use entirely.*) -- to the manslaughter of his wife, Kathleen Peterson.

The primary reason behind taking the Alford Plea is to resolve the murder case that has been going on for over a decade. Neither Michael nor any of Kathleen's family was fully satisfied with the judicial process, and since he was fed up and didn't want a retrial, Michael decided to take a plea but didn't miss a step in claiming his innocence.

In one of his interviews, the 73-year old claimed that he was a victim who had to fight for justice on "a crooked table" where he also had to face misbehaving crime scene analysts and law enforcement officers. Kathleen's sisters were sure that Michael had something to do with their sisters' death; they were upset when the court set him free in 2017.

That same day, Durham Attorney Roger Echols prepared a statement that Mr. Peterson was now responsible for Kathleen's death, and after going through an extensive review of testimonial and physical evidence, he agreed to enter into a plea agreement. The Durham attorney made this decision after consultation with Kathleen Peterson's family and asked a series of questions of Michael in order to make sure that he had no problem with the mentioned terms and conditions.

Conspiracy Theories About The Death Of Kathleen Peterson

This case was fraught with dramatic twists, turns and inconsistencies. Whether it was the wrong report by a blood analyst or different blood patterns than in a usual stair fall, the defense and prosecution teams revealed some interesting yet moving theories such that the direction of the case was completely changed. Their theories ranged from a blood-thirsty bird attack to an extramarital affair revelation, which caused disruption in the couple's lives. From feathers to pine needles, Kathleen's death involves the following crazy and weird speculations, some of which we touched on earlier in the book:

1. An Angry Owl Attacked Kathleen

While following Michael Peterson's trial, one of his neighbors, attorney Larry Pollard, took a step ahead and asked for permission to re-examine the evidence on his own. Upon analysis, he found tiny owl feathers on Kathleen's head along with pine needles in her fist.

Bringing the old findings into limelight once again, he introduced a weird idea that the victim might have been attacked by an angry owl. The bird would have attacked Kathleen instantly and, while struggling to prevent herself from falling, she hit her head on a few steps of the staircase.

Pollard supported his idea by showing similarities of the lacerations of a Barred owl's talons that were caused when she was trying to pull the bird away from her. The jury took his claims seriously and called some ornithological experts for further examination. They also agreed to Pollard's idea; however, the bizarre theory never helped Michael to clear his name from the case.

2. Michael's Extramarital Relationship

During their initial investigation, the police officers discovered Michael's interest in male pornography. They examined his laptop and found a lot of gay adult material along with chats and activities on various escort websites. Upon further probing, they found a male escort named Brent Wolgamott with whom Michael was negotiating for sexual services.

The prosecution also believed that their proof of same-sex infidelity could be the reason for Kathleen's murder because she might have threatened to leave Michael. Here, defending his position, Michael claimed that Kathleen was fine with his relationship, but some sources disagreed by saying that she already left Fred Atwater due to infidelity and, therefore, she wouldn't tolerate his as well.

3. A Supernatural Force, the Mothman, Attacked Kathleen Peterson

There is no doubt that the internet has

been quite successful in involving supernatural objects in creating conspiracy theories. While discussing the Owl theory, some Redditors mentioned that the bird attack was a bit weird considering the size of the feather found on Kathleen's body. They argued that there was something bigger and more dangerous than a Barred Owl; they feared an elusive Mothman! One of the Redditors claimed that:

"While living in the state of North Carolina, one fact was quite certain, that Mothman used to spawn in the surroundings, due to which there were no owls that would have such big feathers. Apart from seeing regular old hawks, there were no such frighteningly large birds that could do such acts."

Someone may be convinced by these claims, but there was nothing that the jury could find mindful and supporting.

4. A Tree Branch was the Murder Weapon

Considering the presence of pine needles and feathers in Kathleen's hair, some people also believed that the evidence might have been transferred by a natural source, i.e., a branch or stick. They believed that this murder weapon would be quite easy to dump. They argued that there were chances for the tree branch to accumulate bits of owl feather. So if this murder weapon was used, there were chances of it having traces of feathers without showing visible signs of it.

5. Kathleen's Life Insurance Triggered Michael to Kill her

Michael and Kathleen Peterson were under a load of debt.

During the trial the prosecution's case focused on money -- or the couple's lack thereof -- as a motive. They argued that Michael's plan to kill his wife revolved around the $1.4 million life insurance policy she had in place.

Despite living what looked like a lavish lifestyle from the outside, the Petersons were in a lot of debt. An agent from the North Carolina State Bureau of Investigation (SBI), Raymond Young, assessed the couple's finances and discovered that they had more than $142,000 in debt spread across 20 different accounts. It was reported that they were spending more than $100,000 more than they were taking home.

Michael's sons, Clayton and Todd Peterson, were also in severe debt. The interest on the boys' loans was so high they had no money left to live on, and their father was concerned. Michael Peterson was so worried, in fact, he emailed his first wife Patty eleven days before Kathleen's death to ask her to take a $30,000 home equity loan to help their sons out because he was unable to do so.

"It would be a huge relief off my shoulders because I am worried sick about them," Michael's email read. *"It is simply not*

possible for me to discuss this with Kathleen."

6. Michael's Sons were the Murderers

In the beginning of the true crime Netflix documentary, *'The Staircase,'* Clayton, Michael's biological son, mentioned the strong and beautiful bond between his father and Kathleen, which makes him happy and jealous at the same time because that bonding was never developed with his mother, Patricia Peterson.

For some viewers, his words were enough to consider him a suspect with a motive of jealousy. Talking about this theory, Todd was presented in front of the jury with the claim that he was already present at the crime scene. The attitude of the two brothers was quite weird and suspicious since one of them refused to say even a word to police.

7. A Rake or Gardening Fork was Used to Attack Kathleen

Since Reddit had been quite active on Kathleen's death speculation, some of the members also thought that the murder weapon would be a garden rake, while for some, the marks look like a three-pronged gardening tool. The discussion ranged quite far and wider than expected, but there is no doubt that the absence of the murder weapon was the most concerning part as there were no proven reasons to find the culprit. However, some Redditors argued that a garden rake might cause parallel lacerations, whereas Kathleen's head had erratic injuries. So this argument came to an end.

8. There is a Curse on the Surname 'Peterson'

Although this conspiracy theory doesn't have scientific support, it is somewhat related to what had happened with Kathleen Peterson. According to some Redditors, there had been quite a lot of spousal murder cases around the world whose surname was Peterson. There was a man named Scott Peterson who murdered his pregnant wife, Laci, while Drew Peterson was found guilty for the first-degree murder of his wife, also named Kathleen. So, considering the facts and details, some people mentioned that this surname had a strange curse on the family.

While looking at these conspiracy theories, one thing quite certain is that true crime fans took a lot of interest in Michael's trial and used their detective skills to make speculations about Kathleen's murder.

Interesting Staircase Facts about Michael and Kathleen Peterson

Although "The Staircase" documentary has been a successful true crime story for the fans, one thing is quite sure: that it didn't focus on Kathleen Peterson herself. All of its 13 episodes were mainly focused on Michael and his innocence, regardless of why he was convicted and the factors behind his trial.

"The Staircase" also left out the following interesting facts about the couple's relationship and Kathleen's death:

1. Kathleen had a high-powered occupation and she was uneasy that she was about to be made redundant. She was Director of Information Services at the Canadian firm Nortel Networks Corporation when she died. According to Beyond Reasonable Doubt podcast, Kathleen was a big earner making a six-figure salary.

In the lead-up to Kathleen's death, Nortel had been making a large proportion of its staff supererogatory -- as many as two thirds (or 45,000 workers). While Kathleen wasn't one of the employees to have been laid off, she reportedly told her sister Candace that she was afraid that by the end of the year she wouldn't have a job.

Michael Peterson mentioned these fears in an email to a family friend just six days before Kathleen's death. "*Poor Kathleen is undergoing the tortures of the damned at Nortel. They've laid off 45,000 people,*" he wrote. "*She's a survivor and in no trouble, but the stress is monumental there.*"

Kathleen died on December 9, 2001, so she never reached the end of the year to find out her fate.

2. Kathleen Peterson was the sole owner of the couple's mansion. The staircase she was found dead at the bottom of was just one of many in the huge property, and the couple were thought to have been relaxing by the swimming pool in the garden prior to Kathleen's death.

But as the prosecution pointed out in the trial, Kathleen was actually the sole owner of the house and the car. Michael may have been a local newspaper columnist and author, but he wasn't a big earner, and he didn't own the 1810 Cedar Street property. He owned nothing. He made practically nothing from his books and depended on Kathleen's income to support him and his sons.

3. Michael Peterson got a pay-out from Kathleen's assets after she died.

As mentioned above, because of her considerable salary, she could afford to take out a hefty life insurance policy which totaled $1.4 million. Within six months of his wife's death, Michael Peterson had collected $347,000 from his late wife's assets to fund his legal defense. Kathleen Peterson's life insurance was later split between her daughter,

Caitlin Atwater, and her first husband, Fred Atwater.

4. Kathleen suffered possible strangulation injuries.

In the last two episodes of *The Staircase*, filmed in 2016 as Michael Peterson's legal case finally drew to a close, you might have noticed the lawyers mentioning "strangulation" injuries discovered in Kathleen Peterson's autopsy. You'd think this would have been a major point of evidence, but for some reason, up until then, it had never been referenced in the documentary series.

Diane Fanning explains the injuries in a little more detail in her book, '*Written In Blood'*. *"Dr. Radisch, the state pathologist, moved her examination to the internal neck area, and discovered a bloodied fracture with hemorrhage on the small extension off of the left thyroid cartilage. It was an injury unlikely to occur in a fall. Usually it was the result of direct trauma to the bone and was common in strangulation or attempted strangulation,"* she noted.

5. Experts believe Kathleen had been dead for some time when paramedics arrived, thus the blood was dry and congealed.

In the first 911 call, Michael Peterson frantically tells the operator that Kathleen is "*still breathing*" and urges them to hurry. But when paramedics arrived on the scene 10 minutes later, Kathleen was dead, and it appeared to them that she had been dead for far longer than just a few minutes.

6.   Michael Peterson had a book deal ready to go if he was found not guilty.

Peterson was a writer, and many said he has the kind of ego which starves for the limelight.

Throughout the weeks of testimony, Michael Peterson had taken copious notes on legal pads. Most likely because he had a book deal with publisher Harper Collins. When the jury found Michael Peterson guilty of first-degree murder in October 2003, the offer was immediately withdrawn.

7.   Michael Peterson ended up dating the editor of '*The Staircase.*'

One thing that absolutely wasn't mentioned in The Staircase is that Michael Peterson didn't remain single for all the years following his wife Kathleen's death. He developed a relationship with Sophie Brunet, the editor of the documentary filming his case. According to the show's director, Jean-Xavier Lestrade, this relationship had no influence on how Brunet edited the series. "*This is one of the incredible things that happened during those 15 years. Life is really full of surprises,*" the director told French publication L'Express. "*They had a real story, which lasted until May 2017. But she never let her own feelings affect the course of editing.*" Yeah, right!

Where are Michael and His Family Now?

After taking the Alford Plea in 2017, Michael finally walked free and began living the life of a common man. Currently, he's still in Durham, in a very tiny apartment. He is working on a new book -- about his own story. Not only the story of the case, but of his life and experience in prison and everything.

However, what most of the analysts anticipate that his new book, if completed, would lead to a lot of controversies. Although he took an Alford Plea and walked free, a lesser number of book readers would be interested.

Patricia Peterson (Michael's First Wife)

After living 20 years with Michael, Patricia still believes that her ex-husband didn't kill Kathleen and he should not be treated the way he is. She had been there for his support right from the beginning. She is now retired and living in Durham.

Caitlin Atwater

At the beginning of Kathleen's murder trial, Caitlin believed that her stepfather was innocent but after seeing her mother's autopsy report, she was convinced by the prosecution's argument that Michael was the real culprit. Her siblings even stopped talking to her after listening to what she had to say about their father. She didn't believe for one second that Kathleen was okay with Michael's bisexuality.

In 2007, she sued Michael for $25 million in the wrongful death settlement and showed anger when he accepted an Alford Plea to the reduced charge of voluntary manslaughter of her mother.

Until today, she hasn't forgiven Michael for her mother's murder and decided to start a new life. She got married to Christopher Clark and began to live outside Durham, after living for a few years in London in the beginning. She is now the mother of twins and known by her new name, Caitlin Clark.

Clayton Peterson

Clayton had been a great support to his father, just like his mother, Patricia Peterson. Right from the beginning until the end, he believed in Michael's innocence. After Michael was released from prison in 2017, Clayton got married to a beautiful girl and started to live in Baltimore. The couple have two children.

Todd Peterson

Just like the rest of the family, Todd also supported his father throughout the trial. After Michael was released from prison, Todd decided to remake his life and began to live in Tennessee with new spirit.

Martha Ratliff

Daughter of Elizabeth and George Ratliff, Martha stood by Michael and declared his innocence in front of everyone. At present, she is living a happy life in Colorado.

Margaret Ratliff

She is the biological sister of Martha who had been living with Michael and Kathleen in their mansion from the time they married. She is quite a reserved and shy person who doesn't like to discuss her personal life in public. She graduated from Columbia College of Chicago and worked on many projects in the film industry as an actress, assistant director and production manager. Currently, she is living in California and known by her new name, Margaret Blackmore.

Epilogue

So what are your views? Was Michael guilty of his wife's murder or is there something that's still hidden? What is your analysis regarding the evidence, the theories about the lacerations on Kathleen's head? Are they telling you a new story? Another person did it and discarded the murder weapon? Maybe it was the Owl? Nevertheless, a jury needs to convict without a shadow of reasonable doubt. But there is doubt. Most people I talk to about this case are 80% sure he's guilty.

Although Michael is out of prison and is living a more private life now, Kathleen's sister, Candace Zamperini, still believes that he was the person behind her sister's death. Is she right or not? There was much more to the case and its proceedings than anticipated. There were a lot of theories that made sense, but still, nothing was proven due to lack of evidence, in my opinion.

Kathleen's murder mystery is still unsolved because people believe the evidence and facts in a different way. Be it the owl theory, Candace's take over Michael's conviction, or anything else, Kathleen Peterson is still waiting for justice!

Do you think Peterson was guilty? Take the *POLL http://rjparkerpublishing.com/the-staircase-the-murder-of-kathleen-peterson.html*

FREE BOOK

ABDUCTION: The Minivan Murders

Introduction

In the world of crime, while each case is heinous and a blow to humanity, there are some cases which leave a mark on not just the victims but everybody who comes across them. The United States alone have been responsible for a few of the most notorious and horrific killers of all time. Ted Bundy, Jeffrey Dahmer and many other serial killers have been caught and convicted for committing gruesome murders and subjecting their innocent victims to torture. A number of the killers who have made headlines across the world have been male, as noted by many psychologists analyzing their behavior. When it comes to female serial killers, there have been several but nowhere near as many as their counterparts. These females have many times worked with a partner, usually male, joining forces to carry out violent acts and torture.

The deadly serial killer couples that shook the world by their grisly and heinous crimes include Michael and Suzan Carson, Doug Clark and Carol M. Bundy, Paul Bernardo and Karla Homolka, and Fred and Rosemary West, just to name a few.

As evident from the above-mentioned twosomes, female serial killers have worked with their male equivalent and gone on to kill several innocent men, women and children. During the 1940s, Raymond Fernandez and Martha Beck, termed as the 'Lonely Hearts Killers', took the lives of three women and a child. The killers' involvement was also suspected in more than twenty murder cases across Michigan and New York.

It surprised psychological analysts and human behavior researchers everywhere that women were partaking in evil acts of violence and pain. After numerous studies between the relationships of serial killer couples, it was implied that the relationship between two partners was somewhat similar to a submissive and a dominant one. Either the male or female was responsible for the execution and torture of the victim, whilst the other scouted possible targets. Despite years of research and studies, analysts were mostly lost for an explanation as to what prompted the serial killer couples to torture and murder innocent people.

While serial killers have been in existence since before the time of "Jack the Ripper", there has been a decline in their numbers over the years. Throughout the early to mid-twentieth-century, America experienced one of its worst criminal periods as far as serial crimes are concerned. The wave continued on to the late 1990s and even into the Twenty-first century. One of the most notorious killing pairs that surfaced during this time was Michelle Michaud and James Daveggio.

Biography

James Anthony Daveggio, also known as 'Froggie,' and Michelle Lyn Michaud were 42 and 43 years of age, respectively, at the time of their conviction in 2002. When news of their crimes made global headlines, researchers and psychologists began to dig deeper into their history and background. It was determined that Daveggio was born on July 27, 1960, in San Francisco, California, while Michaud, also referred to as 'Mickie' by her partner, was a year older than him.

Since an early age, both Daveggio and Michaud encountered difficulties with their family lives, especially during their adolescent years. In 1974, when he was 14 years old, Daveggio was questioned during the investigation of Cassie Riley's murder. The 13-year-old girl was found near an embankment by a creek in Union City, California. Upon investigation, it was revealed that the girl had died due to drowning, and there was evidence of severe assault, with injuries to the head and neck. While rape could not be determined, the investigators found her clothes disheveled. As the case progressed, investigating officials found evidence of James Daveggio being present on the scene when Cassie Riley disappeared. Later on, he even claimed that she had been his girlfriend.

The investigators did not pay close attention to his claims as a few other boys had also gone on record to state something similar. A number of analysts deem this incident the beginning of Daveggio's long violent history. At the scene of Riley's murder, the police found sneaker prints of a size 10 shoe, which helped them come up with possible suspects. Eyewitnesses also stated that, before her disappearance, Riley had been seen talking to a young boy with a green shirt with a sleeve patch. However, this did not lead to any conclusive results. In May 1975, almost six months after the atrocious killing, the police convicted Marvin Mutch of Cassie's murder.

Much later it was revealed that Mutch had been falsely convicted as his prints did not match the evidence found at the scene of the crime nor were any links to Riley determined. Mutch spent 41 years in prison and was only recently released.

Many believe that the reason Daveggio managed to get away unscathed was his sister's false alibi, wherein she stated that her brother had been present at home during the time of the murder. Since that time, his violent behavior began to slowly progress. He would get into fights in his high school and gravely injure his fellow students. He stole a car belonging to a girlfriend's mother and often got physically violent with young girls. Soon enough, Daveggio was sent to live with his birth father in Pasadena, California.

Even that did not make much of a difference, and he was back with his mother after a short stay. He was sent to a juvenile detention center in Alameda County for robbing a gas station. During the detention period, he acquired his nickname, 'Froggie', and also met a friend, Michael Ihde, who shared the same twisted perversions as he did. Most likely, Ihde was the person responsible for triggering his violent sexual fantasies that soon eclipsed his entire thought process. Michael Ihde also went on to become a killer and a serial rapist.

Once out of the juvenile center, Daveggio worsened in his ways. He was known to be involved in several robberies, abductions and rape cases. While initially, the rape charges were dropped due to the victim's statement which could not prove him guilty, Daveggio eventually was arrested and put through a psychiatric evaluation. He was officially considered as a sex offender and flagged by the Sex Offender Registry. However, whenever he moved, he kept his whereabouts hidden from the authorities.

Soon enough, James Daveggio was caught again for picking up a female police officer posing as a prostitute and offering her money. He was sent to the California Medical Facility, situated within Vacaville, and fined heavily for drinking and disorderly conduct. Despite that, Daveggio managed to secure his release shortly and moved to Sacramento. He dropped out of high school and then married his pregnant girlfriend, Becky. The relationship did not last long due to Daveggio's habitual gambling and heavy drinking. In Sacramento, he joined a motorcycle gang called The Devil's Horsemen. It is commonly understood that during his time in Sacramento, James Daveggio, met Michelle Michaud. These future serial killers bonded over their mutual appreciation of violent sexual acts.

Michaud, at the time, was already a prostitute and frequently experimented with various drugs. After a string of failed relationships, Michelle Michaud was his first steady partner. As experts determined, Michaud also came from a similar background as Daveggio and might have been assaulted by her father. At the age of 16, she had run away from home and moved in with a physically abusive drug dealer. Michaud entered prostitution and took multiple partners before meeting Daveggio. She was apparently impressed with his position as a gang member, believing herself to be protected in his presence. Prior to their meeting in 1996 or 1997, Michaud had worked in a massage parlor and had been arrested several times.

Michaud and Daveggio established a relationship with the latter moving into her house after a short period of dating. She tried her best to impress him but, after a while, nothing was good enough. However, Michaud stayed with Daveggio and even tried to build a family with him.

The bar where he worked was robbed just before Christmas and, while his involvement in the crime was not proven until later, he was fired for getting violent with the customers. After that, he took a job in security, working as a guard during the day. His interest in Michaud began to decline, and he would often bring other girlfriends to the house.

Daveggio's partner allowed the presence of various women in his life, believing that it would keep him happy and content. Despite that, his behavior began to worsen, and he became increasingly violent and abusive towards Michaud. He would often lock her up and leave her for days, all the while subjecting her to physical violence and savage sex. Both Michaud and Daveggio were into drugs, and their expensive habit soon created a mountain of debt for them. In order to lessen the financial burden, they let their friend deal drugs from the premises. Soon enough, their luck ran out. The authorities discovered that their home was a place of illegal drug activity. During the law enforcement investigation, Daveggio's status as a sex offender was discovered and, as there were children in the house, he was ordered to move out.

At this same time, Daveggio was also kicked out of The Devil's Horsemen due to his involvement in a burglary. Accordingly, this was when he began to exhibit curiosity in serial killers, reading books about them and being particularly fascinated with Gerald Gallego. Drawing inspiration from Gallego, Daveggio managed to persuade Michaud to kidnap her daughter's friend and lure her to an isolated place. He assaulted and raped her, while his partner was also involved in the act. This was the beginning of the crime spree the deadly killers were about to commence.

Soon after this incident, 20-year-old Alicia Paredes had been walking home one night when a green minivan stopped. Froggie hopped out while Mickie was at the wheel. He grabbed Alicia and tossed her in the van. Daveggio raped her while Mickie looked on. They then tossed her out like a sack of trash. Alicia went directly to the police. Paredes had heard him refer to Michaud as 'Mickie,' and she worked with a sketch artist to identify the criminals. While it was determined that the driver was female and the abductor male, the investigating officials still came up short of arresting the perpetrators.

The green minivan belonged to Michaud and soon became a torture chamber for her partner. He installed hooks and ropes in the vehicle, removing the seats to accommodate his gruesome criminal plans. Both Michaud and Daveggio began to play out their perverse fantasies, kidnapping more women and forcing them to participate in sexual acts. The duo's further victims included Michaud's daughter and five other girls across the state of Nevada. Psychologists and analysts across the globe failed to identify the root cause of this increasingly violent behavior which terrorized the victims.

Daveggio did not even spare his own 16-year-old daughter, who told a grand jury that on Thanksgiving Day 1997, her father asked if she would like to help kidnap a victim off the street and kill her. He called it "hunting", she said.

During their spree, Michaud was apprehended by police on charges of falsifying checks and booked into the Douglas County Jail in November 1997. She was released shortly; however, after which the two went on to resume their activities. While her stint in jail had brought her onto the radar of the authorities, both she and Daveggio escaped arrest until the rape and murder of Vanessa Samson on December 2, 1997.

The police began to investigate the two more thoroughly, taking statements from Michaud's daughter and her friend, both of whom were rape and assault victims. While the officers managed to get a location on the couple, they failed to make an arrest. One by one, victims were discovered, yet at the time, Vanessa Samson had not been killed.

As an arrest warrant was issued for both Michaud and Daveggio, the couple made their way into Pleasanton, California. Daveggio's desire to kill kept becoming stronger until he finally asked Michaud to bring him a victim. Unfortunately, 22-year-old Vanessa Samson caught the eye of the deadly twosome and was subjected to physical assault, rape and torture. Her body was dumped over an embankment. Soon afterward, the authorities tracked down the killers to a motel and managed to arrest them on charges of assault and kidnapping for starters.

At this time, Vanessa Samson's body had not been discovered. It wasn't until ropes and other evidence of the crime surfaced that the investigation took a turn.

The serial killers were linked to a possible murder and then Samson's body was discovered. They were both charged with rape, torture and murder. After a trial, Michaud and

Daveggio were sentenced to death while analysts grappled with the acts of 'pure evil' that they had perpetrated. The relationship between the two became a subject of many studies with psychologists trying to figure out which was the dominant and which was the submissive. Numerous accounts were taken and pieced together, eventually leading to the conclusion that both were equally involved in the assault and torture of innocent victims, including their own family members.

Later on, when they were finally apprehended by the police and details of their case began to make rounds, more information regarding the background of the killers surfaced. Daveggio had always tried to emulate his father, and according to one of his wives, idolized him in every sense. His father had multiple failed relationships and married quite a few times. While this way of life worked out for him, Daveggio could not keep himself from spiraling out of control. He displayed sociopathic tendencies from an early age and was unable to keep away from trouble. It was evident to the people around him that James Daveggio did not care about anyone and lacked self-control when it came to interacting with the opposite gender.

Perhaps the lack of a father figure in his life was a huge factor in his behavioral problems. It was also the reason why, despite his frequent run-ins with the law, he was always protected by his mother, Darlene. As a teenager, Daveggio would get into trouble in his neighborhood for displaying violent behavior or getting caught up in a burglary, yet Darlene always came up with an excuse to prove him innocent. For her, James Daveggio was a harmless child who had minor problems while growing up.

Further on, when the rumors began to circulate that he may be involved in several abductions and physical assaults, Darlene still managed to convince herself that her son could not be at fault.

One of Daveggio's classmates remembered him as a boy who did not stand out amongst the crowd at first glance. She recalled that he was a 'shy and quiet boy' who had bright blue eyes and blond hair.

While in high school, Daveggio managed to keep his twisted sexual fantasies hidden and even attracted a few girls. However, this was a short-term phase that quickly ended when he made the move to Pleasanton. He constantly rebelled in his new school and failed to make any new friends due to his increasing aggressiveness. It was in a juvenile detention center that he met Michael Ihde who truly connected with Daveggio like no one ever had before. Ihde shared the same dark fantasies and penchant for violence as him, prompting a strong bond between the two.

Both Ihde and Daveggio began to spend their time together and, soon enough, their influence rubbed off on each other. With the progress of time, Daveggio moved away and joined the biker gang, while Ihde went on to become a serial rapist and murderer.

After going on a spree in Bay Area, California, Michael Ihde was finally caught and charged with several murders of young women. It was during his conviction that Daveggio's name surfaced and their connection became known to the authorities. However, at the time, Daveggio was still active as a gang member and only involved in petty crimes. The police kept him on their radar as a sex offender but did not pursue him due to lack of evidence.

Daveggio's life changed when he met Michelle Michaud, but it is unclear as to who was the driving force behind their murder and rape spree. A few psychological experts have shed light on the possibility of Daveggio suffering from a personality disorder. They say that there were two personalities that Daveggio was caught in between: the shy and quiet one, and the other loud mouthed and aggressive side. It could have been Michelle's entry into his life which prompted his aggressive personality to become prominent and eclipse his rational thought. However, at the end, the argument can be made that Daveggio was a sociopath from the very beginning. Michaud might have helped him execute his twisted plans later on, but it was only a matter of time before his violent side got the better of him.

The backseat of the minivan was removed and ropes were attached inside to restrain their victims

Michelle Michaud

There are varying accounts of how Michelle Michaud and James Daveggio actually met. One popular version of their meeting describes Michaud running into Daveggio at a bar in 1996 and becoming instantly attracted to his biker gang status as well as muscular looks. It has been stated that when Daveggio joined the gang, he got heavily tattooed, dyed his hair and stole a Harley Davidson to become initiated. Michaud was working as a high level prostitute when she walked into a bar, Bobby Joe's, with a friend and took one look at Daveggio, who was a bartender there, and announced that she 'wanted him'.

While this account could very well be true, Michaud later contradicted this version and narrated the story of their first meeting herself. According to her, she met Daveggio on Halloween in 1996. They were introduced through mutual friends and met to discuss some problems her daughters were having with some friend of his. Daveggio stepped in and assured Michaud that he would speak to the man involved and 'take care' of the problem. It was implied that due to his increasingly aggressive streak, he might have done much more than just talked to the man involved.

Soon afterwards, Daveggio became interested in the fiery red head, who at first rebuffed his advances. She told him that her work had introduced her to the worst in men and she no longer wanted to be with one. Michaud also spoke openly about staying in her line of work and not wanting to change whatsoever. Despite that, Daveggio pursued her and insisted that they see each other. After a short while, she relented and they began to date.

Michaud did not expect it to become anything serious; however, against all odds, she found herself falling for him. He treated her like a lady and did not bring her background as a prostitute up again. While most of his teeth had been knocked out, Michaud found him attractive and was drawn to his blue eyes. Daveggio somehow managed to charm her with his mannerism and muscular build which provided Michelle with a sense of security. Despite her aggressive demeanor, Michaud craved protection and security that she lacked since an early age. It was implied that her father could be the reason behind her going into prostitution and she had never had a childhood while growing up.

Perhaps the couple's tumultuous family background had been a major factor into bringing them together. In the early days of their relationship, Daveggio earned Michaud's respect and acceptance. He stood on her behalf against family members and friends who constantly shunned her for her lifestyle. At the same time, Daveggio also managed to drive away the people who warned Michaud of his aggressive and violent nature.

There were a few people in Michelle Michaud's circle of friends who told her that James Daveggio was not good for her. Just like his third wife, Donetta, she also did not listen to the warnings of her friends and family. She had become so enamored by him that minor indiscretions on his part did not matter to her anymore. According to one of her statements, he was the kind of man who demanded 'respect from your family for you.' She also said that Daveggio stood up to her family and did not let anyone chase him out of her life which showed his commitment to her and their life together. Michaud stated that 'he had been nothing but good to her.'

At first look, the two could not have been more different in their demeanor. Right from his school days, Daveggio had managed to subdue his true nature by appearing shy and quiet to girls during initial meetings. He had very deep blue eyes that also made him come across as someone who was engaging and slightly attractive. Michaud, on the other hand, was a strong-headed, loud-mouthed and self-confident woman. There was nothing even remotely shy about her, and she could most probably walk into any room with ease.

The people who initially came across the couple did not think of them as a likely match. Michaud was a well-dressed and well-spoken woman while Daveggio did not pay much attention to his words or attire. He would dress up in worn-out clothes and biker boots as Michaud carried herself in a way that was completely different to her way of life. Her self-confidence was very evident in every interaction, which was a striking contrast to Daveggio's visible discomfort within a crowd.

Analysts and psychological experts say that, much like Daveggio, Michaud could also have been suffering from a multiple personality disorder. When amongst people, her ladylike, champagne-loving side would be prominent, but the underlying loud-mouthed and aggressive personality was always there. Later on, a few close friends of Michelle Michaud went on record to say that, despite her conservative dressing and sophisticated manner of speaking, she never shied away from describing her sex life in graphic detail.

As opposed to her open and outspoken verbal interactions, Daveggio was closed off and never talked about his sexual preferences in front of anyone. Whenever he was approached by a woman, he would quietly move away. It was assumed that his need to be in control was such that a woman making the first move on him turned him off.

After meeting Michaud, Daveggio could not help his attraction towards her. They may have been different in outward appearances and demeanor, but it can be said that ultimately they were cut from the same cloth. At thirty-seven years of age, Michaud was an attractive woman with an athletic body. Both her mind and appearance attracted Daveggio from the very beginning. She was an intelligent and sharp woman who exuded self-confidence as well as poise. Michaud would talk openly about her sexual desires and fantasies, often speaking about how she would like to interact with her partner. Evidently, Daveggio and Michaud connected over similar sexual preferences.

It was quite surreal that a well-dressed and well-spoken mother of two could spin such dark carnal fantasies that could leave the listener speechless.

Appearance-wise, there was no surprise that Michelle Michaud managed to make heads turn. With dark red hair and striking green eyes, she attracted men everywhere she went. Her family moved from one place to another before settling down in South Sacramento. Little is known about her early life, as contradicting accounts surfaced during the trial. According to some versions, her family appeared outwardly middle class and fairly normal, while others hinted towards disturbances and frequent misdemeanors.

However, all accounts stated that, beginning in her teens, Michaud started to rebel against her family and all figures of authority in her life. She dropped out of school at the age of fifteen and began a relationship with a boy who already was on the run from the law. Michaud soon began to experiment with drugs and forayed into prostitution. She ran away from home and bounced from one location to another before coming across James Daveggio in Bobby Joe's.

The twisted pair soon formed a fairly strong bond that led to Daveggio moving in with Michaud after just a short period of dating. Whilst Daveggio's interest in his partner began to fade gradually, Michaud did everything she could to keep them together. She even allowed him to fraternize with various other women and suffered physical abuse as well. Their terror spree which went from California to Nevada began soon after he was fired from his job at the bar. Daveggio turned Michaud's minivan into a torture chamber and raped several victims inside.

His partner was responsible for luring them in and occasionally participated during the act as well. It boggles the imagination of analysts and psychological experts everywhere as to what prompted Michaud to become a murderer and serial kidnapper. While she may have been booked for run-ins with law as a rebellious youngster, there was little which implied that she would go on to lead a life of full-blown crime. During her spree with Daveggio, she was arrested for the second time in her life for writing bad checks but was let out shortly. Once out of police custody, they started moving again, taking the van around and targeting innocent victims across various cities, even crossing state lines.

The relationship between the two has been the subject of many studies and books. Authors have tried their best to identify the dynamics that Daveggio and Michaud built upon. While the connection may have been inspired by twisted sexual fantasies, the murder element came in much later. Michaud may have known about her partner's violent nature and aggressive streak, choosing to adapt to his way of life. Soon enough, her sociopathic tendencies rose above and broke through the seemingly poised demeanor. In her reign of terror, along with Daveggio, she left behind a trail of scarred and traumatized victims.

During the trial, Michaud was also termed as 'pure evil' and many believed that the death penalty was the only appropriate justice. The heinous crimes for which both Daveggio and Michaud were responsible had left the whole country reeling in shock. It was presumed that the perpetrators felt little or no remorse for their crimes, as Michelle Michaud was known for openly boasting about their violent escapades and was constantly planning on upping the stakes in their criminal offences.

A witness called to the stand by Michaud's attorneys implied that her behavior was a reflection of the abuse and violence she might have suffered at the hands of various boyfriends early in her life. It was also claimed that her father may have raped her and thus prompted her decision to become a prostitute. Despite evidence of Michaud's father's innocence being presented in court, the defense continued to push for a psychological evaluation. However, at the end, justice prevailed and the federal jury handed out a death sentence to both Daveggio and Michaud.

Michelle Michaud has been a notorious criminal who will be remembered in the years to come. Many police officers and behavioral experts have conducted numerous studies and research on Michaud's background and history so as to come up with any explanation behind her erratic decline into the abyss of darkness. Some cite Daveggio's influence as a defining factor that led to Michaud becoming one-half of America's most vicious serial killer couple, while others say that the underlying dark side was already present and waiting to surface beyond the calm exterior. Her personality disorder was such that to passersby she seemed like a woman of great taste and striking looks. Michaud was well put together and at first glance was like any other native of California. There are accounts of her being hospitable and helpful on various occasions. According to one narrator, Michaud usually chose to stay away from sanctimonious people and was not a devout believer of any faith or religion; however, she did come to admire Father Kavanagh.

The priest gave numerous sermons and lessons at the church in Michaud's locality and somehow managed to make an impression on this rebellious girl. It was alleged that he became a prominent figure in her life and even watched over her on countless occasions. Apparently, her time with Father Kavanagh stayed a memory with her for a long time as she helped missionaries and church delegations that came by her house. It has been related that once a Mormon missionary group stopped at her house and were so impressed by Michaud's sincere and generous behavior that they offered her free painting services. While they painted her house, she prepared delicious meals as a token of appreciation for their free service.

The few accounts of Michelle Michaud's early days are all reminiscent of her rebellious days. She was always a free-spirited girl with little regard for rules and regulations, yet there was nothing so dark that could signify that the girl would go on to become one of the country's most hunted criminals. She had fairly good relations with a few family members and always had a number of friends despite the chip on her shoulder.

After dropping out of school, she had gone through a number of bad relationships that perhaps added to her erratic behavior and internal instability. The man she moved in with at the age of sixteen was a drug dealer and had been investigated by the police numerous times. Due to her relationship with him, Michaud began to experiment with hard drugs and ventured into dealing as well. Her first run-ins with the law occurred in 1991 when she was working at a massage parlor in Sacramento. The police raided the establishment that was supposedly a place for 'relaxation' but actually was covering a number of illegal activities from drug dealing to solicitation.

She was arrested along with other workers on the premises and released after serving a short sentence. Soon after her release, she changed locations and moved around constantly until Daveggio came into her life. This was a turning point in both of their lives, and they went on to become a deadly serial kidnapping and murdering duo who claimed the lives of several innocent women.

Spree of Terror

Analysts say that Daveggio was already a sociopath and his tendencies were fueled by Michael Ihde's influence. Michaud could have been propelled into joining the world of crime by her partner who was already bordering on psychopathic aggressiveness. Daveggio appeared like any other man to an onlooker but was masquerading his true nature beneath a slouchy and quiet demeanor. According to researchers and investigators, Daveggio was smiling slyly in his yearbook which could have been an early sign foreshadowing his perverse fantasies.

Michaud, on the other hand, was only involved in minor offences and prostitution before she met Daveggio at Bobby Joe's. Their relationship was twisted from the initial stage. While Daveggio managed the bar, Michaud was frequently heard relaying her dark and violent sexual fantasies to anyone who would listen. She would talk about her previous sexual encounters as well as anything she would like to do with her partner in the future. While outwardly, Michaud and Daveggio seemed polarities apart, they did have similar interests as far as sexual fantasies were concerned.

As their relationship progressed, things took a turn for the worse. Daveggio began to drift away and started taking multiple partners while Michaud held onto him, believing that if she let him live his way, he was going to come back to her. Soon enough, he was fired from the bar for his erratic behavior and constant fights with the customers. The couple's financial situation began to deteriorate, which was why they invited Daveggio's friend to sell drugs from their house. This was one occasion where luck did not side with the two; a police bust was carried out and all operations were halted.

Due to Daveggio's sex offender status, he was ordered to move away from the residence as there were children in the house. This was the time when his killer instincts began to completely take over his thought process. He began to take a keen interest in serial killers, especially Gerald Gallego. As the information came to light during the trial, Daveggio had already been charged with the rape of three women before the actual partnership was struck. He had been fined and arrested for soliciting a prostitute and offering alcohol to a minor girl. Prior to meeting Michaud, Daveggio had quite a rap sheet that included assault and various cases of abuse.

He was also using methamphetamines heavily and had a string of bad relationships. Michaud on the other hand was only arrested on accounts of prostitution before she met Daveggio, with her next conviction being for fraud after their relationship had begun.

After her partner was fired from his job, Michaud became the sole breadwinner in the household. However, her business also took a severe hit when the drug abuse became a huge problem that prevented her from procuring clients. With so much less income to go on, the deadly team decided to explore possibilities. Daveggio, being greatly inspired by Gerald Gallego, tried to convince Michaud to join him in his evil plans just as Gerald did with his partner, Charlene. Analysts have stated that this was perhaps the point when something snapped inside Michelle Michaud.

Her brain was so addled by the drug abuse that rational thought no longer prevailed. Daveggio soon managed to convince her to lure over their first victim, her daughter's thirteen-year-old friend. The girl became the couple's first victim of rape but somehow escaped with her life. This was just the beginning of the pure terror that was going to be unleashed upon unsuspecting victims.

Community college student Alicia Paredes was walking home from a night class one evening when a green minivan stopped near her. She was abducted by the serial killing twosome and raped. Michaud and Daveggio let her go and did not kill her. Paredes reported the incident and worked with a sketch artist to get their sketched likenesses developed. However, luck was on the criminals' side, and they evaded any persecution or arrest for the time being. Paredes only caught the name

'Mickie' as she had heard the man calling out to the driver. Despite that detail, the police did not come up with any conclusive evidence of the crime or the perpetrators.

They went from one location to another, targeting victims and raping them. Somehow, the two managed to evade the police despite Michaud being arrested for a short period of time on account of bad checks due to her rising debt. Once she was out, the crime streak continued with Daveggio making several modifications inside the van, installing various tools that could be used to subdue the victims. The pair drove around Reno, Nevada, and took Juanita Rodriguez as their next victim. She was the one who put them on the map for investigating authorities in Reno.

While the couple released her after sexually assaulting her, they threatened her life if she ever told anyone about the incident. Terrified, Rodriguez went to the authorities and narrated her ordeal. During the incident, she had somehow managed to catch the mention of the name 'Mickie' vaguely. She passed on the information to the authorities who began to work on the case co-coordinating with the police in California where similar incidents had occurred. The name 'Mickie' had surfaced twice thus far, but there was no evidence of the perpetrator to whom it belonged. Both Daveggio and Michaud managed to evade any persecution or arrest and continued their crime spree without interruption.

They struck again soon after Rodriguez, this time in Sacramento. Seventeen-year-old Patty Wilson was the next victim who was tortured and raped. She was picked up by Michaud and lured into the minivan under the impression that they were going to experiment with some drugs together. After assaulting her, both Daveggio and Michaud contemplated killing her; however, she begged for her life and vowed to lie to the police about the incident. After driving around for a few hours, Wilson was let off with a threat that if she told the truth to anyone, she would be dead. The terrified girl knew that the couple was armed and very dangerous; they even knew where she lived.

When the authorities questioned her, Wilson made up a fake story and stuck to it despite the police suspecting fallacy. However, by this time, the authorities across Reno and California had enough to put together a case. Rodriguez had given a description of her male assailant, and the police had managed to come up with a sketch of the man. The woman driver could not be identified as the victim was unable to get a closer look at her. In a surprising twist of fate, it was Juanita Rodriguez who helped spur the chase of the serial raping and killing for the authorities. Michaud had not even imagined that Rodriguez would remember the details of her perpetrators. Although deeply traumatized, she relayed as much information as she could to the FBI investigators.

As the victims began to traverse across

state lines, the Federal Bureau of Investigation was brought into the investigation. Special Agent Lynn J. Ferrin immediately went to work, along with his team of detectives and criminalist Renee Romero. The criminalist was well versed in DNA samples and evidence checking, which is how he discovered that the male assailant who assaulted Rodriguez had either undergone a vasectomy or suffered from a medical condition.

While evidence collection was going on, Michaud and Daveggio struck again. This time the victim was a family member who also became a prime witness in the investigation later on. On November 18, 1997, a Sacramento police officer received a call that two girls had been molested and assaulted by a couple in a green minivan.

This was perhaps the beginning of the end for the serial killers. Baker revealed the names of the assailant and even confirmed that she heard Michaud admit to the rape of Juanita Rodriguez. The officer who took their statements looked up the names against previous charges and discovered that both Michaud and Daveggio had been arrested more than once. Upon further questioning, the whereabouts of the lethal pair remained unknown as they were living in their minivan and constantly moving from one place to another.

However, this was considered a major breakthrough in the case as the police now knew whom they were hunting for. Despite the efforts of the authorities and investigators, they could not prevent what was about to happen next.

The horror that unfolded on December 2, 1997, will go down as one of the worst setbacks in the progress of humanity. While Samson's murder led to an end of the three-month-long crime spree, it also reminded the people that there was an endless pit of darkness, which could have claimed any one of them. Vanessa Samson was a native of Pleasanton, California, where Daveggio had spent most of his adult life. The duo had returned to the town as it seemed target-rich around Thanksgiving. Parking their minivan near a high school, the serial killers went out looking for their next victim. Temporarily, they were forced to move away as a teacher caught them around campus and raised an alarm.

During this time, an arrest warrant was issued for both Michelle Michaud and James Daveggio in multiple cases of assault and rape. Yet the authorities closed in a little too late. They could not save Vanessa Samson's life as she became their next and final victim before they were arrested by the police.

The couple had become more and more erratic due to heavy drug abuse. They were making mistakes, which led the police toward closing in on them by the minute. As the chase was on, Daveggio decided that he could wait no longer to find the next victim. He sent

Michaud on a lookout again and proceeded to purchase various tools that he would use to torture Samson before killing her.

While Vanessa Samson's murder is what led to justice being served, it was the information given by Rodriguez which led the authorities to two of the deadliest criminal's at the time. They not only raped several innocent victims, but as the case progressed and more details came forward it was revealed that their involvement in various other abductions and assaults was also possible. Speculation arose that both Michaud and Daveggio had been behind the disappearance of Jaycee Lee Dugard with a witness putting the former at the scene of the crime.

There were a few unsolved cases, which could well be closed if they were connected to the victims, and it looked very likely they had taken more victims than the ones who had come forward.

During their trial, it was established that the couple had raped and assaulted six known victims, all of them young girls. The crime spree was such that it spared no one who was deemed a suitable victim. As investigators delved into the details of each crime, they unraveled more horrors. It was evident that the pair was one of the deadliest criminal partnerships to have struck across the country.

Before Daveggio and Michaud, the Federal Bureau of Investigation had come across a similar couple who wreaked havoc within the same vicinity. The Sacramento and Nevada authorities could never forget Gerald and Charlene Gallego, both of whom were responsible for the sexual torture and murder of eleven girls. Daveggio had, in fact, been inspired by the serial rapist and killer. Studying Gallego's crime spree during the 1980s, the authorities found striking similarities between their victims and those of Michaud and Daveggio. Just as Gerald Gallego had convinced his partner Charlene to get on board with his gruesome and vicious plans, James Daveggio followed suit. He brought out the worst in Michaud, and her darker side eventually took over.

She joined her boyfriend on a long spree of torture, assault, rape and then murder. While the serial raping and killing couple drew comparisons with Gerald and Charlene Gallego on the basis of a similar mode of operation, they managed to leave their own mark on the criminal history of California and Nevada.

In the late 1970s, Gerald Gallego came across Charlene at a poker club in Sacramento and the two soon began to date. Both were into recreational drugs and did not shy away from a wild experience every now and then. After living together for a short span of time, Gallego began to find their sex life dull and monotonous. His partner did not excite him anymore and thus began his search for something more stimulating. Whether Charlene was aware of his sexual fantasies from before is unknown; however, the investigation did bring to light details of Gallego's violent sexual preferences.

Drugs played a very important role in the couple's lives and fueled Gallego's erratic behavior. When Charlene got pregnant, Gerald Gallego decided that it was time to put into play his twisted fantasies. He convinced his partner to lure over innocent young victims so that he could satisfy his raging desire. Both Charlene and Gallego would scout targets at various places such as malls and restaurants, after which the former would invite them in under false pretenses. They too operated out of a van where Gerald Gallego would torture and assault his victims.

Their murderous crime spree claimed the lives of eleven innocent girls, who were also subjected to sexual slavery. After raping and murdering two teenagers in California, Gerald Gallego found himself being pursued by authorities as their bodies were discovered at a farm where he had been seen by a witness. Soon afterwards, Gallego's daughter also came forward with a molestation claim against her father. While an arrest warrant was issued for him, the police did not find the murderous two till after they had left a trail of eight more victims in their wake. They constantly were bouncing from one place to another, which made it difficult for the authorities to track them down in the 1980s.

Finally, Gallego and Charlene fled to Reno, Nevada, and married under an alias. 1984 was the year which saw the deadly killing duo caught and convicted after claiming numerous victims in California and Nevada. After their trial, Gerald Gallego was sentenced to death for the atrocities committed while his partner Charlene was awarded prison time. The jury determined that, in light of all the facts and evidence, the woman had been a mere pawn in Gallego's evil schemes and had not actually participated in the torture or sexual acts. Hence, she was handed out a sentence for sixteen years and eight months in a Nevada prison.

Analysts and investigators found that, when it came to choosing their victims and torturing them, James Anthony Daveggio and Michelle Michaud mirrored Gallego and Charlene. The serial raping and killing of Daveggio and Michaud went after unsuspecting young girls from California and Nevada. While they only murdered their last victim, the assault and physical torture inflicted upon the other girls was very similar to Gallego's method.

Despite that, James Daveggio and Michelle Michaud could not have been more different than Gerald and Charlene Gallego when it came to relationship dynamics. Most psychological experts were of the opinion that Michaud was the dominant one in the partnership. Whilst Charlene had played the role of a bystanding accomplice, Michelle was an equal partner in every sexual assault which had been carried out.

According to a statement made by the investigating officials from the Federal Bureau of Investigation (FBI) later on, it was the 'first of its kind' case where a woman partner had "allegedly taken an equal role in a series of sexual assaults." Charlene Gallego was merely an 'enabler' but not Michelle Michaud, who could never be pushed into the background by a man. Daveggio and Michaud's seventeen-year-old victim Patty Wilson somehow confirmed that when she was lured into the van and captured; her assailant was, in fact, Michaud and not Daveggio since he could not perform at the time.

Further details surfaced and revealed that Michaud was the one who threatened all their victims before letting them go. She would warn them not to go 'somewhere alone' because they wouldn't be 'so lucky again' the next time. The young girls would be absolutely terrified and would refrain from even telling anyone the details of the incident. It was already established that Daveggio and Michaud carried a weapon with them, which had been witnessed by both Patty Wilson and Juanita Rodriguez.

The other victims also knew that they were armed and could kill them at any time, which is why the young women usually complied with their acts of atrocities. Juanita Rodriguez recounted the ordeal to the authorities later on, and her sheer terror was evident in each detail. Unfortunately, this was one thing that she could never erase from her mind. The incident had to be retold quite a few times: to the medical staff at the hospital who examined her with a standard rape kit procedure to gather evidence, then to the detectives, as well as the federal authorities. Rodriguez had to relive the horrors of that night more than once, and that thought alone was enough to send shivers down everyone's spine.

However, despite the terrible ordeal she went through, Juanita Rodriguez's bravery was what led to them being eventually captured. Detective Desiree Carrington of Placer County was key to closing this case. After meeting Rodriguez, she knew immediately that they were not going to stop at one victim and that the police department had another Gallego-like case on their hands. Carrington was very understanding and sympathetic towards Rodriguez's ordeal, but she knew that no matter how traumatic the rape incident, every minute detail had to be collected. Preserving any sense of modesty on the victim's part would only hurt their investigation and allow the man and woman to roam free.

Carrington, her partner Bill Summers and FBI agents immediately went to work around the area looking for any evidence or suspicious people. The investigating teams knew that time was of the essence as they realized the pair could strike anywhere and at any time. Special Agent Lynn J. Ferrin, who had come across a lot of these cases during his long career in law enforcement, recognized that solving the case was not going to be an easy task. After hearing about the rape incident, Agent Ferrin had wasted no time in contacting Juanita Rodriguez and conducting an extensive interview with her.

Rodriguez told him that the couple had several personal items and sleeping bags stashed away in their van. This was one factor that worried Agent Ferrin somewhat as he realized that not having a permanent address made it all the more challenging for the authorities to track down the assailants. The couple were on the move constantly and could be anywhere across state lines. However, the agent was very well trained in handling violent crimes, particularly Title 18 offences that focus on abductions and sexual abuse. He knew that he would have to inspect every nook and cranny to find this deadly couple.

Juanita Rodriguez revealed that whilst she was desperately trying to keep herself alive, she attempted to engage the couple in conversation to gain their sympathy. She said that the man had a fondness for one particular Johnny Cash song. When she asked what it was based upon, his reply chilled her to the bone. Her male assailant described the song as being one about a man who shot and killed a man from Reno just so he could 'watch him die.' Rodriguez instantly knew that she could meet a similar fate if she didn't do something fast.

She made up a story and lied that her nine month old baby would be alone in the world if she was killed. Somehow, the woman assailant took mercy upon her and decided to let her go. Rodriguez was warned not to turn around and to keep walking for twenty minutes. Analysts and investigating authorities assessed from the details she revealed that Michelle Michaud was the dominant figure in the couple's relationship. Juanita Rodriguez had stated that when the man got tired of abusing her, he seemed almost remorseful but was very clear that he did not mean to 'take her back' as she might 'do something stupid.' However, after she kept on begging and promising that she wouldn't, he turned to the woman driver to ask what they should do with their victim; surprisingly, she said that they should 'let her go.'

Similar to Rodriguez's ordeal was Patty Wilson's night of horror. She had been lured into the van by Michaud under the pretense of doing a 'line of meth' together. Wilson was already familiar with the man and woman as she had seen them around the area quite a few times. However, what followed was something that she could not have imagined even in her most fearful nightmare.

As soon as she entered the green minivan, Wilson was punched by Daveggio and knocked out cold. Much later, she recalled the physical impact of the hit, which caused her to 'see stars' and pass out for almost five minutes. While the perpetrators subjected Wilson to assault, the male assailant could not perform sexually and backed out of raping her. The terrified girl recounted that she had told Daveggio how the entire ordeal was reminiscent of her stepfather's abuse. Apparently, this killed the man's mood and he moved away. However, Wilson still had much more to endure. The man called out to the woman, who wanted 'her turn' since he wanted nothing to do with her anymore. Hence, the girl was subjected to rape at the hands of the woman driver after she parked the minivan in the hills near Livermore, which is a town close to Pleasanton, California.

By the end of the ordeal, Wilson was almost convinced that she was going to die. The couple had stated that they could not drop her back to where she worked as it could be risky. They did not want to end up in jail.

She begged them to let her go and promised that she would lie to her manager, making up a false story as to what happened. Wilson told them that her manager would call the authorities as she was not the kind of person to take off from work like that, and when the police came, she would lie to them as well.

The couple drove around contemplating

what to do and finally decided that they would let her go. However, the false story came from them. Wilson was told that after she went back, she would say that three teenage boys kidnapped her from the parking lot of the gaming arcade where she worked. She also had to elaborate that the boys raped her at the hills and then dropped her off. Patty Wilson agreed to everything and in return was let off at a gas station situated on Dublin Boulevard. She called the manager from the gas station and repeated the exact same story about being raped by three teenage boys.

While her manager believed the fake story, the Dublin police who had been informed of the incident found it greatly distorted. They were skeptical about its authenticity but did not manage to get anything further from seventeen-year-old Patty Wilson. The girl was well aware that her assailants were deadly; she had seen a gun in the passenger seat as well. She knew that the couple had her residence details and could kill her at any time if she revealed any mention of them.

There was no doubt in her or the authorities' minds that this was a dangerous, armed, and out-of-control pair of serial rapists. Nobody in their path was safe, and until they were caught, everything had to be done to keep the victims safe.

The Events of December 2, 1997

Much has been said and written about the events leading up to and on December 2, 1997. This was when finally they claimed the life of an innocent 22-year-old girl, Vanessa Lei Samson. The horrors are such that neither the authorities and nor the victim's family and friends will ever be able to suppress the incident's memory. This was the time when investigating officials and the police were already closing in on the two. Their crime spree had continued across the states of Nevada and California, but the authorities were now finally on the trail of the suspects.

Vanessa Lei Samson

An arrest warrant had been issued for both Michaud and Daveggio. From September to December, the deadly couple had taken five known victims, and Vanessa would be their sixth.

It was as if nothing mattered anymore. All hell had broken loose.

Vanessa Lei Samson was a lively and cheerful young girl who still lived with her family and was close to all her siblings. She was studying at the Ohlone College and saving up for further tuition. Her hopes and dreams were brutally snatched away from her as she became James Daveggio and Michelle Michaud's latest victim. However, unlike the prior ones, Samson was not lucky enough to escape with her life.

By picking out Vanessa Samson, the couple changed from their usual victimization. They did not abduct her from a dark alley or in the night from a far-fetched place. Surprisingly enough, her kidnapping occurred in the morning hours and within a fairly populated area.

James Anthony Daveggio and Michelle Michaud were on the lookout for a new victim. Later, in the trial, it was revealed that the sadistic couple termed their excursions as 'hunts' and 'adventures.' Michaud described the rapes and torture inflicted upon each victim as an 'adventure,' while Daveggio chose to refer to the escapades as 'huntings.' It was evident that they both found it quite thrilling.

The couple had been scouting the grounds of a high school in Pleasanton,

California, when a teacher found their presence suspicious and they were forced to move away. It was presumed that they chose such places as they were target-rich and young girls could be easily picked up without raising any alarm. By an unfortunate twist of fate, Vanessa Samson showed up on their radar, and what followed was one of the most brutally executed crimes in the history of the United States.

People who are familiar with the area of Pleasanton, California, describe it as being a relatively safe and close-knit community where previously such crimes were unheard of. The Samsons were like any other typical all-American family, enjoying a quiet life in the suburbs. It was Thanksgiving time, and the family had all gathered together to celebrate the occasion. The mother, Christina Samson, was overjoyed that all of her family had come together to spend time.

Her children, Vanessa, Nicole and Vincent, along with her husband, Daniel, would finally be able to get away from all the hassle of work, study and other activities for a short while. It was going to be a good, relaxing vacation for the Samson family. However, things took a turn for the worse just a few days after the holidays ended. Unknown to the family, they were already in town and had claimed an innocent victim in an area not far away from where they lived.

Just a week prior to Vanessa Samson's

murder, the couple, who had checked into a motel, abducted and assaulted a young teenage girl. The victim later recalled that both Michelle Michaud and James Daveggio had stated something along the lines of attacking another girl next. She admitted that Daveggio had raped her and then let her go. However, she had heard him saying that the holidays would make up for the biggest 'shopping days of the entire year and would be best for killing somebody.' The authorities discovered that, just a few days later, the pair were on the hunt for their next victim.

This one would not be so lucky. The couple drove around various markets and went to Hayward Kmart where they purchased curling irons and duct tape. Their van, which also served as a torture chamber, was fitted with ropes and other tools that were used to subdue the victims. Michelle Michaud and James Daveggio took their purchases to a Motel 6, situated in Pleasanton, and checked into Room 137. On November 30, 1997, they were spotted outside the motel with Michelle Michaud's green minivan being parked outside.

The police who were rushing against time to catch the serial raping and killing couple revealed that they stayed close to Foothill High School where it was easy to scout potential victims. On the very same day, Daveggio and Michaud were also caught on tapes within an adult toy shop. They made various purchases, including a cassette of a pornographic video titled 'Submissive Young Girls.'

On the fateful day of December 2, 1997, Vanessa Samson was about to go to her job she had landed just a few weeks before. At 7:30 in the morning, she stepped out with her lunch and backpack, bidding farewell to her mother. Samson was already used to walking short distances and did not mind the walk from her home to the offices of SCJ Insurance Services. Her sister, Nicole, was staying with a friend and had offered her a ride to work that day; however, she had not responded back so Samson had chosen to walk.

It seemed as if nothing was going right for her that day. An unsuspecting Samson walked on Singleton Street and then onto the road that would intersect Kern and Page courts, leading her to Gibraltar Drive. This was when she heard the wheels of a van crunching past her. For about a minute, Samson did not pay any attention to the green minivan until it turned around and stopped right in front of her. A man stepped out and dragged her inside.

Roofers working at a nearby house heard a loud and desperate scream, which was quickly muffled. A green minivan was also spotted driving away.

What happened with Vanessa Samson includes gruesome details of torture and continuous abuse, after which, despite being told that she would be let off, she was brutally murdered. As it was revealed later, Samson was strangled by a rope and her body dumped near an embankment. Her body was discovered half-frozen a couple days later, by which time the two had already been apprehended, but their involvement in her murder was unknown.

The police had caught the couple at their motel and arrested them on charges of assault and abuse. However, since the whereabouts of Vanessa Samson were still unknown, the truth about her murder was yet to surface.

According to case details, it was revealed that Vanessa Samson had been tied with a rope and repeatedly assaulted for almost half a day. She had been tortured with the cords of the curling irons and other tools that the couple had in their minivan. After the assault in the van, they brought their victim to the Sundowner Motel at South Lake Tahoe. They checked into Room 5, and nobody spotted anything suspicious. It was revealed that this was the motel where Samson's abuse and torture carried on for long hours.

She may have been told that she could go free when the couple took her along Highway 88, but the brutality knew no end. Samson was strangled with a rope and her body was dumped in the snow on an embankment. The police later found it in such a terrible condition that nobody would be able to forget it for years to come.

Vanessa Samson was a girl who was loved and adored by one and all. Her family and friends were in a frenzied state of panic when she failed to report to work and return home. Her coworker knew that it was not at all like Samson, who had hardly ever been late to her job, to not show up at all. She immediately informed the family who began a search for their beloved family member.

Her friends and family called up every known acquaintance and hospital in the area but could not obtain any knowledge of her safety. The last anybody had seen of Vanessa was her walking out the door for work. Christina Samson had a horrible 'sinking' feeling in her stomach, yet she hoped and prayed for the best. Her mother wanted to believe that she might have gone to visit her close friend, Raul Guilliarte in Davis; he was supposed to come down during the holidays but had not been able to make it. However, all her hopes were shattered when Guilliarte revealed that he had neither heard from nor seen Vanessa Samson.

As time passed, Samson's friends and family became increasingly disturbed. They were almost certain that something terrible had happened to her. Vincent, Samson's brother, took off from his job in San Francisco and organized a search party for his sister. He even took help from the authorities and had fliers posted. Yet all of this was to no avail. Vanessa Samson had been dead for many hours, and her body was lying cold in a nearby area.

Vincent Samson felt directly responsible for his sister's disappearance and wanted to do everything that he could to find her. As the details were revealed later, he believed that he had failed his sister at the time. Despite everyone's best efforts in finding Vanessa Samson's trail, nothing could be turned up. Her assailants were already in police custody and charged with rape and assault. However, Samson's death was still not linked to them.

On December 4, 1997, Vanessa Samson's body was discovered and the police began investigating. Along the way, it began to look like the murder could be connected to the pair. They had been examining the objects in the couple's minivan, and things were getting more suspicious with each discovery. As the police and investigators stripped down the van, they found various tools of torture, a few of which had blood on them that looked fairly fresh. Vanessa Samson had already been missing for two days, and it was looking more like a certainty that these two were directly involved in her kidnapping.

After her body was discovered, the police and investigating officials found evidence that indicated that she was murdered by one or both of the killers. Vincent Samson was the first to be notified of his sister's unfortunate demise. A trucker had spotted the body at 10:45 a.m. on that fateful day, and later on Vincent Samson was the one who had to break the news to his family. He told the police that all that was going through his mind at the time was he will have to deliver such news to his family, which was going to alter their lives in every possible way.

When he arrived home, his mother, Christina Samson, instantly knew that something was wrong. Her daughter had been 'taken away' and nothing was going to be the same again.

Later on, during the investigation, she said that 'a part of her died' that day, and she was going to cry over it for the rest of her life. Her precious daughter, who had held so much promise, was taken away brutally and made to suffer immensely due to no fault of her own. Vanessa Samson had only been the 'pretty girl with black hair' who suddenly caught the eye of the burly, bearded man with several tattoos. Daveggio then made his partner turn around, pick her up and force her into the van. The only mistake that the unsuspecting girl had made that day was to walk to work.

The Investigation and Arrest

After brutally torturing and assaulting Vanessa Samson, James Anthony Daveggio and Michelle Lyn Michaud drove around Highway 88, possibly looking for a dumping ground. They settled on an embankment and, after tying and gagging her, Daveggio strangled her with a black nylon rope that the couple had purchased a few days before. Before selecting Vanessa Samson as their next victim, the two had already decided that they were going to take it up a notch in their crime spree.

The police were hot on their heels and closing in, while drugs and methamphetamines were spurring their erratic behavior more so than ever before. Their green Dodge Caravan had been spotted in the parking lot of the Motel 6 in Pleasanton; hence, it was only a matter of time before someone reported it.

Despite the investigating authorities being so close, they could not manage to save Vanessa Samson's life. There was perhaps a chance that the couple may have escaped the police for a longer time, even after murdering Samson. However, a mistake on Michaud's part was all it took for the police and detectives to corner them and take them in. Michelle Michaud was due for a court hearing in Sacramento on account of her being indicted for writing bad checks. She was supposedly going to meet her mother on the way as well.

On December 2, 1997, just a few hours after Vanessa Samson's murder, Michelle Michaud made the grave error of stopping to collect her welfare check. She also made a trip to a check cashing store and was instantly spotted by the local police. While she continued on her way to South Lake Tahoe, where her hearing was scheduled at a nearby court, the authorities were informed immediately.

The police followed the trail to Lakeside Inn, situated within Stateline, Nevada. Officers had questioned her mother, who also gave up her daughter's whereabouts, and they were able to pinpoint a location. A young girl had also come forward with the information that she had been the couple's victim in a minivan that was very similar to the one parked outside the motel's casino. Special Agent Ferrin led the hunt, ordering all the police officials to spread out and cover as much ground as possible. The parking area, restaurant and casino were all swept thoroughly and, within minutes, the police arrested Michelle Lyn Michaud from Room 133.

James Anthony Daveggio was playing slots at the casino and was instantly handcuffed and taken away as well. They were charged with assaults and kidnappings at the time, pending a trial which sentenced them for these crimes in 1999. The police were definitely relieved that after a month-long chase, they had finally caught these two monsters who had been terrorizing people across California and Nevada.

Yet more horrors were about to unfold. As the investigating team examined the van and each piece of evidence in detail, they discovered a few objects that were indicating something sinister. The authorities had already started to investigate any possible links to the couple and Vanessa Samson's murder. It turned out that Michelle Michaud, who was being held in Douglas County Jail, saw the news about the 22-year-old's body being discovered off Highway 88, and she blurted out to a friend of hers in prison that they might be responsible for it.

The authorities immediately began to question her further until she waived her rights and started answering their questions. During her interviews, she mentioned Vanessa Samson quite a few times and appeared to trail off while recalling some of the details of her kidnapping. Her behavior indicated that she was involved in Samson's kidnapping and definitely a murder suspect. The authorities spurred their investigation further and tried to find evidence which could possibly connect the two to Samson's abduction. The team soon came across the gags, bloodied ropes and white towels, evidence of a struggle.

They questioned Michaud again and she revealed that one of the gags had Samson's saliva on it as neither she nor her partner had wiped it off. The police soon found it along with a curling iron that had a severed cord and duct tape. Everything was sent to the laboratories for testing, and the results shocked everyone.

The curling iron was bloody and contained other bodily excretions as well. It was revealed that the tape also carried Michelle Lyn Michaud's right thumbprint. There was obviously no doubt in anyone's mind that they had made the authorities' worst fears come true and claimed the life of an innocent victim.

Vanessa Samson's murder was what led to the couple being handed out a death sentence. Their act was referred to as 'demonic' and 'vicious' with Vincent Samson openly addressing James Daveggio and Michelle Michaud in court and referring to them both as nothing but evil. There was no doubt that the death penalty was justice served and this twisted couple deserved nothing less.

Police and investigating officials were astounded by the gruesome details as they came to light, with some even stating that the notorious couple was a 'match made in hell.' Daveggio and Michaud had inflicted torture and abuse on all of their victims, going to another level of extreme with Vanessa Samson. While they had managed to evade the police on countless occasions, Pleasanton, California, was the end of their crime spree.

The police across Nevada and California began to search for the couple after identifying them. Investigating officials had already started building a case against a male-female team of attackers in Reno when Juanita Rodriguez reported her rape and assault at the Placer County Sheriff's Department. While the sketches were somewhat hazy, the police across the two states were on alert and looking out for any such suspicious couple. At the time, luck somehow sided with Daveggio and Michaud, and they managed to keep themselves out of sight.

After hearing the victims' accounts, the police hastened in their efforts to catch the rapists. The law enforcement agencies had seen first-hand the carnage that the two had left behind. It now became even more certain that this couple was unhinged and capable of the worst.

Investigating officials finally tracked down the couple and cornered them in Pleasanton, California. At that time, the charges against them consisted of assault and rape. When Vanessa Samson's body was discovered, the police began to search for the perpetrators. This was when the Daveggio and Michaud case became a murder investigation. While the former's mate had brought the information regarding her involvement in the murder, it wasn't until two days later that the evidence proved what everybody had already assumed. The news report had mentioned that the murder weapon was a black nylon rope. Michaud saw this and started to fear that she was going to be implicated once the police found conclusive proof.

After long, intensive interviews, the officers managed to put together a clear picture. The woman had claimed that there was some evidence of the murder on a few tools and torture objects found in the van. As it turns out, she was right. James Daveggio was also questioned and it was learned that he had indeed repeatedly assaulted and then murdered Vanessa Samson by strangling her. While Michaud later contested her statements, the jury and court held fast to her testimony and even brought it to Daveggio's trial.

She was sentenced to death for murder and found guilty on all counts of rape and assault. Her partner met the same fate, and eventually, the twisted two were separated from each other. Michaud was transferred to federal custody and assigned attorneys. Eventually, the two were handed over to Alameda County where a grand jury indicted them for the abduction and brutal murder of 22-year-old Vanessa Samson. During the course of their trials in 1999, they were also handed out sentences for assaults and rapes across Nevada and California.

Perhaps their sentencing gave closure to their victims who had been waiting for justice to be served. The terrified girls who had been afraid to come forward mustered the courage to open up about their suffering to the authorities. Some of their victims testified in front of the jurors at the trial. Patty Wilson, who had been scared into silence until their arrest, finally made her story public. She revealed the atrocities committed against her when the couple kidnapped her from the parking lot and then later threatened her to force her to lie.

As further evidence surfaced, it was claimed that Daveggio, who was already a registered sex offender prior to meeting Michaud, might have been involved in a few other rapes and killings before going on the crime spree with his partner.

Trial and Further Details

The arrest of Michelle Michaud and James Daveggio may have brought peace of mind to the authorities, but there was a lot more still to come. Vanessa Samson, who had been reported missing for two days, was found dead with visible marks of abuse and torture. Once it was proven that they were behind her murder and assault, their five-year-long tedious trial began. The death sentence was justly handed out, and the family of the victim had some satisfaction in that the killers of their beloved family member got what they deserved.

However, during the trial, there was nothing but pain and difficulty for not just Vanessa Samson's family but also the couple's numerous rape victims. The girls who had suffered abuse at the hands of Daveggio and Michaud had to recount the horrific details of their ordeal and relive it. Meanwhile, Samson's family and friends had to sit through the court proceedings which focused on the torture and abuse that the girl had to endure before she was killed so brutally.

Christina Samson and her husband stated that they would forever be 'haunted' by what happened to their little girl. The mother also said that she was going to mourn her daughter's death every day as her suffering was so great that it could never let her live in peace. Vanessa 'Ness' Samson was 'defenseless and alone' as well as 'frightened beyond words.' During the court proceedings, Vincent Samson addressed James Anthony Daveggio and placed a framed picture of his sister beside him.

He reminisced about his sister right from her childhood days, remembering the times he used to pay her to wrap Christmas presents. Vincent Samson also recalled the beautiful and responsible adult she had grown up to be, caring for everyone and never backing out of a commitment. All of Vanessa Samson's family and friends jam-packed the courtroom while the trial lasted, and they always showed up wearing purple ribbons to commemorate Vanessa Samson's memory as it was her favorite color.

Vincent Samson also questioned Daveggio, stating that what could he possibly say to a person who 'raped, molested and killed' his younger sister. He referred to him as a 'demon' who had committed 'vile' acts against innocent children.

The brother of Vanessa Samson was not the only man referring to the monsters as vicious and vile in open court. Alameda County Superior Judge Larry Goodman, who handed out the death penalty sentence, also referred to the incident of Vanessa Samson's murder and brutal torture as 'cruel, senseless, vicious, and depraved.' He stated that the death penalty was indeed appropriate for the heinous crimes for which they were responsible.

On the day of the sentencing, the dark and morbid tale of the slaying and torture was narrated by the jurors one last time. Just before the proceedings began, Vincent Samson expressed his confidence that 'justice was going to be served.'

While recounting the details of the murder, Alameda County Senior Deputy District Attorney Angela Backers stated that the duo had 'promised' Samson that they were going to let her go just like the victims prior to her. However, after driving around the area, they decided upon a murder site and eventually strangled her with a six-foot-long nylon rope.

The District Attorney told the jury, comprised of five men and seven women, that Vanessa Samson's murder capped the couple's six-victim spree that had spanned over a couple of months. They had subjected young innocent girls to abuse and sexual assault, not even leaving their own daughters unharmed. Backers presented the discovered evidence in court that included the pornographic video from the adult shop, a book about serial killers entitled 'The Dead of Night,' bloodied curling irons with Michaud's fingerprints on the duct tape, and a pack of serial killer cards. She stated that the couple was mostly inspired by the Gallegos with the cards featuring both Gerald and Charlene prominently.

Their rape and abuse of victims followed a similar pattern to the notorious criminal serial killing and rapist couples of the 1980s. Backers further said that the couple had probably upped the stakes and progressed to murder as they also aspired to have their pictures immortalized in serial killer cards, just like the Gallegos.

The initial arrest was made in the case of Juanita Rodriguez's assault in Reno, where Michaud pleaded guilty and was sentenced to fifteen years, while Daveggio was handed a twenty-five-year sentence.

The District Attorney added murder to the charges, thereby convincing the jury to recommend a death penalty.

Michaud initially contested the terms of her sentence, but the court dismissed all such objections and proceeded as scheduled. The forty-three-year-old and her lover were being investigated jointly by the Federal Bureau of Investigation and Placer County Sheriff's Department for assault and kidnapping. The police officials tracked them down to a motel in Stateline, Nevada, and isolated the two, arresting them on the premises.

In a twist of irony, the Sheriff's Department had secured the arrest warrant on the very day Vanessa Samson was abducted and murdered, December 2, 1997. When Special Agent Ferrin ordered his team to secure the area and lock the place down, he strategically planned the arrest. Michaud claimed in her appeal that her arrest had been on unlawful grounds and hence she was challenging her conviction.

One of the agents in the team was sent up to Michaud's room, claiming to be the hotel manager and asking her to come outside as her boyfriend needed assistance. This was a way to bring Michelle Michaud out and arrest her. In reality, James Daveggio had already been found at the slots and taken into police custody. Soon after, his partner also met the same fate. Once Michaud was surrounded by the law enforcement officials, she was quietly apprehended and taken into another hotel room where the agent cuffed her to the chair.

Special Agent Ferrin got Michaud to sign consent forms for searching their vehicle and read out the Miranda rights to her. She waived them and was sent into an interview room where FBI agents and Place County Detectives were waiting to question her. However, once in the room, she asked for the bathroom, immediately halting the interview. Michaud was booked into the Douglas County jail in Nevada on counts of possession and hardcore usage of controlled substances. Meanwhile the police searched inside the Dodge Caravan and came up with more evidence of suspicious activity.

Based on that, a warrant was issued for Michelle Michaud on charges of aiding, abetting and kidnapping. Just a day after the discovery of Vanessa Samson's body, Michaud saw a police report which implied that, upon investigating, the authorities had been able to narrow down the suspected murderers. After seeing that, Michaud was in the cell with Teresa Agoroastos, her mate, and became increasingly disturbed that she was going to be in so much 'trouble.'

The cellmate contacted Deputy Douglas Conrad and asked him to come over and talk to Michaud. He ordered the women to come to the front of their dorm, after which Teresa Agoroastos revealed that Michaud had information regarding a murder. While the distraught woman remained silent and neither confirmed nor denied her mate's statement, Conrad took the matter further and informed his supervisor, Sergeant Arnie Digerud. Upon his instructions, Conrad took Michaud into a holding cell and waited for Sergeant Timothy Minister and FBI Agent Christopher Campion to interview the woman.

Agent Campion turned on the recorder and asked Michaud if she was aware of what was happening. He questioned whether she really did want to talk to him about a murder which had been bothering her and whether she would like to have an attorney present. After hearing her Miranda rights, she again waived them and submitted to further questioning. The interview lasted around nine to ten hours. Campion returned with Placer County Detective Desiree Carrington who had pursued the case relentlessly and made the arrest in her jurisdiction. After two more days of interviewing, Michaud was handed over to federal custody and prosecuted accordingly.

She was charged with kidnapping and transportation of the victims across state lines into Reno. Michaud raised objections to her conviction, but the appeal was rejected by the courts and her sentence was upheld.

Once again, she argued that her arrest had been unlawful due to incriminating circumstances. She stated in her appeal that the agents who had asked her to open the door of her hotel room violated her Fourth Amendment Rights. Her argument also covered the investigation in the Placer County jail. She said that her distressed state of mind blurred out any objectivity and she may have made the wrong statements.

The court rejected all of her arguments and stated that the ruse employed by the police to get her to come outside was justified as an arrest warrant had already been issued. While as far as those statements were concerned, the details were not clear and led to a murder investigation, at that point the circumstances had changed.

Both Michaud and Daveggio were separately arrested and taken into custody individually. As the court proceedings began, the twosome did not cross paths again. Michaud's testimony was used in Daveggio's trial but, other than that, it was the end for the murderous demons.

The investigating officials were unable to comprehend how two twisted individuals had managed to evade the authorities for so long. Their spree was heavily influenced by drugs, lust and an out-of-control rage on the part of Daveggio. It was by pure luck that they escaped arrest and managed to claim several victims in their wake.

Authorities across Nevada and California had been on the lookout for a couple in a green minivan but, despite numerous attempts, had failed to capture them. Ultimately, their arrest came after the murder of Vanessa Samson who had to give up her life for the couple to end their reign of terror. As the court proceedings revealed, the meeting of these two evolved into something very dangerous.

Michaud was a high-level prostitute, while Daveggio was a recognized sex offender who also worked with a gang. There was nothing good that could come out of their union. Nobody really knew what attracted them to each other. Michaud, from an early age, was the kind of individual who defied all social norms and went after what she wanted. The confident redhead was the kind of woman who was rarely turned down.

After getting together with Daveggio, she realized that he was highly unstable and she would not hold his interest for long unless she gave in to the abuse and his outrageous demands. Soon enough, she became the torturous, murdering woman who was handed down a death penalty. It was as if every moral fiber in her was compromised by the overwhelming desire to keep her partner pleased. It progressed to a stage where she initiated and actively participated in the abuse.

Psychologists believed that Michaud definitely liked assaulting and raping the innocent victims. The sexual motivation is actually a huge factor which kept the couple going from one place to another, scouting for victims and then subjecting them to physical and mental trauma.

James Daveggio, on the other hand, was a sociopathic disturbed individual since a young age. His past girlfriends and wives claimed that their loved ones had warned them about Daveggio's volatile temperament. Throughout adulthood, Daveggio had been involved in various incidents which indicated that a life of crime awaited him farther down the road. Despite receiving several warnings from the police officers, Daveggio did little to find an alternate path. He was absolutely convinced that darkness was his destiny and nothing could change that.

His firing from the job and removal from the gang, The Devil's Horsemen, gave him plenty of time to obsess over the twisted sexual perversions he carried around. He brought Michaud in as a partner on his journey of crime, convincing her that they could become the next Gerald and Charlene Gallego.

Regardless of their background and life experiences, nothing could justify the offenses for which they were proved responsible. Their respective attorneys may have argued for a lighter sentence and tried to defend the criminals, but it was evident that the only suitable justice would be capital punishment. When a witness brought in by Michaud's attorneys claimed that she had been abused and traumatized as a young girl, the state argued that this couldn't possibly be true as her father had been a military man with a strong character. Michaud had moved with her family like every other family in the forces from one place to another, settling down in a middle class neighborhood in California.

It was alleged that, despite gaining stability in her family life, she was getting restless. Michaud wanted to keep moving and, in order to do so, she made the decision to quit high school. The teenager then somehow forayed into prostitution. It was presumed that as a young girl with striking good looks, Michaud was aware of the effect she had on men. She also believed herself to be of a higher intelligence and astute observation, which is why her outlook on everyone around her was dismissive. According to Michaud, she did not want to be around such 'immature' people.

Psychologists and analysts examined the relationship between Daveggio and Michaud very closely. Once all the case facts and victims' testimonies came to light, it started to become clear that, whilst starting out, Daveggio was the one calling the shots, his partner quickly took over.

The notorious couple was compared constantly to Gerald and Charlene Gallego, who had even subjugated their victims into being 'sex slaves.' It was Charlene who was responsible for choosing the victims and luring them over to the van where Gerald Gallego would be waiting with a weapon. However, that remained the only common aspect between the two serial raping pairs.

After the Gallegos were caught, the case evidence which was presented implied that Charlene was not an active participant in either raping or assaulting the victims. In this case, there was Michelle Michaud who didn't back away from torturing or holding the victims down in all of the rapes, abductions, and then murder as well. There were instances when she chose the victims, lured them over and assaulted them subsequently. The authorities noted that this was a one-of-a-kind case where the female in a serial killer relationship was as much responsible for the abuse as her male counterpart.

Analysts concluded that, considering her personality from the beginning, it was no surprise that Michelle Michaud turned out to be the ruthless killer that she was. Since she was a teenager, Michaud had become heavily dependent on hardcore drugs, including methamphetamines, and was often under their influence. Her experience with various men had taught the woman how to hold her own. Unlike her partner at the time, Michaud managed to keep the inner turmoil subdued for as long as she could. Her outward appearance did not from any angle give away her profession or hint toward the instability she harbored.

When she and James Anthony Daveggio became romantically involved, they seemed like an odd pairing. While in the beginning, Daveggio might have been the 'bad' influence in her life, at the end, it was clear that Michaud had been enabling her own dark side all along. She dominated the relationship, taking over the acts of torture and making moves that previously were unheard of by a female perpetrator.

It also became evident that she had no remorse for any of her crimes. During the court proceedings, James Daveggio was asked by Vincent Samson, the victim's brother, if he had felt any guilt or remorse over his act. The grieving brother questioned Daveggio about the murder and whether he felt apologetic for the committed crimes. Vincent Samson did the same thing during Michaud's hearing.

The court allowed James Anthony Daveggio to respond to Vincent Samson just before he was to be sentenced. The forty-one-year-old, who was wearing the bright red jail attire, turned and faced the family of his unfortunate victim. He stated, "I, in fact, did not kill Ms. Samson. By law I am as guilty of her death as Michelle is." Daveggio went on further to say observing Vanessa Samson's family and realizing the love they had for her made him feel horrible about what he had done.

He looked at the 22-year-old's friends and family and admitted that he 'had never seen such love' before in his life. Daveggio closed his statement by acknowledging that he thought about his actions every day and does feel remorse over them. Michaud on the other hand, adhering to her attorneys' advice, did not respond to any statement or make a comment.

Vanessa Samson's mother, Christina Samson, spoke about the irreparable damage her daughter's death had caused in their lives. She stated that her daughter had a lot to live for. Her friends spoke about how she brought joy into a lot of people's lives and nothing would ever be the same again.

Before the sentence was given out, Nicole Samson, the victim's sister, was questioned outside the court about the possible punishment for the killers; she stated that it was 'in the hands of the jury, the judge and God.'

Sentencing

In September 2002, Michelle Lyn Michaud and James Anthony Daveggio were sentenced to death by a jury consisting of four men and eight women at the Alameda County Superior Court. The jury decided upon a death sentence for the couple in the light of all the evidence of torture and rape in twenty-two-year-old Vanessa Lei Samson's murder.

Throughout the proceedings, both the law enforcement agencies and the state prosecutors emphasized that it would be the right outcome considering all the atrocities. The verdict came after a long wait for the family of the victim. Despite the fact that capital punishment is frowned upon across the country, this was one case where perhaps nobody protested against it. Everyone was sympathetic to the plight of the dead girl as well as the other victims.

The question in the minds of the people was, how could anybody possibly do this to an innocent girl? During the sentencing hearing, the state prosecutors revealed that Vanessa Samson had almost averted the couple, but Daveggio made his partner turn around so he could pick up the beautiful young girl walking by herself.

On the day the penalty was given, Alameda County Superior Court Judge Larry

Goodman presided over the proceedings of the court and announced the final verdict. The jury responsible for the conviction raised the possibility of capital punishment in June. After the decision had been read, Judge Goodman went on record to say that he agreed with the jury and it was the right thing. They had been responsible for a heinous crime that was unfathomable in all ways.

The couple was sadistic and absolutely merciless, which ultimately led to the argument that no mercy should be shown toward them. Both Daveggio and Michaud had ensured that there was no way Samson could have been rescued or found alive. During the assault and torture, she had been forced to wear a rubber ball gag so she could not call out for help or make any noise.

The gruesome details which came forward led the jury to recommend the death sentence for the couple. Initially, James Daveggio and Michelle Michaud had been arrested on account of rape as they had been found responsible for assaulting a young girl in Reno. As more victims came forward, the Reno case proceeded to the U.S District Court where Michaud was eventually sentenced to confinement. Daveggio was brought up on the same charges with double counts of rape as well as assault.

During the Vanessa Samson murder and rape trial, the Reno victim, along with the couple's previous targets, agreed to testify in front of the jury. They were going to recount the details of what had happened with them so that the court could come to an adequate decision in the case of Samson's murder.

Throughout the proceedings, Vincent Samson had strong faith in America's justice system. He knew that his sister's death was not going to go unpunished and even stated in open court that Daveggio 'deserved to die.' On the day of the sentencing, the courtroom was filled with Vanessa Samson's friends and family members. Deputy District Attorney Angela Backers had led the prosecution side and presented key evidence that ultimately resulted in the jury deliberating over a death penalty for two days and finally handing it out.

Backers told the jury that the two found gratification in their crimes. The rapes and murder was regarded as a cat-and-mouse game where the two sought the thrill of torturing their victims until they grew bored. As it was in Vanessa Samson's case, the couple was looking to switch things up a bit and escalate from rape to murder. Law enforcement agencies had recovered the saliva-stained gag as well as the bloodied curling irons from the minivan where Samson was restrained. Angela Backers established that both of these tools were used as torture instruments to subdue and rape the victim.

James Anthony Daveggio and Michelle Lyn Michaud were convicted of first degree murder under special circumstances, murder in the commission of rape, on May 6, 2002. Soon afterwards, the jury decided to recommend a death penalty for the gruesome murder and rape by instrument. The decision was spurred by further revelations that Vanessa Samson had been the sixth victim in a series of brutal assaults that had lasted a span of three months and crossed state lines. The unfortunate girl was their only murder victim, but five others had barely managed to escape.

After the sentencing, Michelle Michaud became the fourteenth woman to await her execution on death row in California. She was taken to the women's quarters within the female prison at Chowchilla. It is expected that Michaud will spend the remaining time confined in this jail.

A Psychological Profile

The serial raping and killing of James Anthony Daveggio and Michelle Lyn Michaud drew interest from psychological experts and profilers across the country. This was a case that stood out amongst America's crime history. The acts of torture they had subjected their victims to were gruesome and incredibly brutal. While the victimization was similar to Gerald Gallego and other serial killers in the past, Michaud's role in the crime was what captured the attention of the law enforcement agencies as well as psychological analysts.

Before Vanessa Samson's case, there were no reported cases of rapes or assault where the perpetrator had been a woman engaging in the act. While there had been male-female serial killer couples in the past, the woman was mostly submissive in the relationship, with her part restricted to luring in the victims.

However, Michelle Michaud changed the way serial crime teams would be regarded in the future. She not only initiated the sexual torture and assaults, but she also dominated her partner. It was deduced from victim testimonies that Daveggio usually left the decision making to Michaud. He also let her take charge of the situation, be it driving from one town to another or choosing a target.

Juanita Rodriguez recounted to the authorities that when she was begging to be let go alive, she appealed to the woman, making up a false story of being mother to a nine-month-old baby. According to Rodriguez, the woman seemed sympathetic after asking a few questions and realizing that there was a child who needed to be looked after. When Daveggio asked her what they should do with the victim, Michaud appeared to deliberate for a minute and then finally decided to let Juanita Rodriguez go.

As was evident from the girl's traumatic account, between Daveggio and Michaud, the latter was in charge of making important decisions, such as what to do with the victims in the end. Like Rodriguez, there were other victims who also had similar stories to share. The common factor in all of those was Michaud's increasingly aggressive streak.

In seventeen-year-old Patty Wilson's case, Michelle Michaud was the assailant as well as the ever-present looming threat that forced the young girl to stick to the fake story she reported to her manager and the police. When Wilson agreed to lie about what she had endured that night, Michaud ripped the girl's shirt to make it appear real. The woman had taken to criminal life like a fish to water. She knew how to terrify the victims and make sure that they remained silent. While Daveggio incurred the violence physically, Michaud traumatized them emotionally.

Her threatening, raspy voice remained with each of the victims long after they had been dropped off. Psychological experts concluded that Michaud was indeed very much in control of the situation and did not consent to just being in the background. She wanted to be as much a part of everything as Daveggio; in fact, her urges were even more powerful than his. Wilson stated that it was Michaud who had come up with the false story and had torn her shirt for effect, making it clear that the woman assailant did not shy away from any challenge. This made her all the more dangerous and fearsome.

The conflict in her personality was such that it boggled the minds of analysts and profilers. They failed to pinpoint the exact cause of the turmoil or isolate any one factor which caused her to take such a turn. The question remained, did she suffer from a multiple personality disorder or was she a ruthless sociopath all along, hiding beneath a polished façade?

Who was Michelle Michaud really?

Nobody could actually come up with an answer to that question, other than what had already been determined. In the eyes of the world, she had begun as a well-paid prostitute whose actions were initially the result of methamphetamines and other hard drugs. As a young, rebellious girl, she went through several failed relationships with abusive partners, finally finding her place with Daveggio. The tattooed gang member gave her the home life she may have always aspired to possess. She may have realized that she would not do better than him and, hence, made it her life's aim to keep him happy and satisfied at all times.

At the very beginning, Michaud was the submissive partner that Daveggio always wanted. However, once she ventured into the world of crime, she became aware of her potential. The woman would no longer settle for keeping her partner happy. Their spree was as much about her fulfillment as it was his.

Her role as a mother was also keenly observed by the experts and analysts. While she may not have been a model mother, the accounts of her earlier life implied that she did take care of her young daughters and looked after them. All that changed drastically when Daveggio entered her life. It was as if her motherly instincts were completely eclipsed by her desire for that man. She let his drug dealer friend set up shop in their house despite the presence of her children.

One of the duo's earliest victims was a 13-year-old friend of Michaud's daughter. Nancy Baker later stated that Michaud forced her into the room where Daveggio was waiting to rape her. She later joined in as well. While her partner might have been detached from the victim, Michaud herself knew the girl quite well. Baker visited their house frequently and was on close terms with the family.

Her progression has been charted by analysts who claim that the victimization of Nancy Baker was symbolic to her fading rationality. She lost all ability to connect or empathize with anyone. It got to the point where her own daughter's suffering pleased her.

Yet somehow, Juanita Rodriguez's appeal managed to sway her. Once she found that their victim might be a mother, Michaud decided to let her go. It could be the last remaining shred of humaneness that prompted the decision or just an error in judgment since Rodriguez was the victim who played a huge role in the couple's arrest on account of rape and assault in Reno, Nevada. Experts and profilers also believed that Juanita Rodriguez's release was only made possible because they did not have any plans to kill their victims as yet.

Michelle Michaud's personality was one of the most perplexing contradictions that the psychological and criminal experts had come across.

It was unanimously agreed upon that there was no emotion or remorse involved in the decision to let any of their victims go, especially as far as Michaud was concerned. While Daveggio may have expressed his remorse during one or two of the early encounters, his partner was completely devoid of any display of guilt or weakness. In the beginning of their spree, one of their victims stated that Daveggio even seemed to apologize for hurting her and causing the trauma but quickly overcame his emotional admission as Michaud diverted his attention to the problem of dealing with their victim.

As the crime spree spiraled out of control, it claimed several victims, who all appeared as easy targets. Daveggio and Michaud usually chose girls who were on their own and abducted them from sparsely populated locations. Vanessa Samson was the only victim taken from an area where possible witnesses could have been present. It seemed as if, by the end, Michaud was beginning to enjoy the acts of torture and abuse more than her partner. When her daughter was calling out to her for help, she warned her to 'keep quiet' and ordered the girl to submit. Experts and analysts were of the opinion that she became sexually aroused during the incident.

As the details of all the rapes and assaults unraveled, it was almost no surprise that the couple had killed Vanessa Samson in such a brutal and vicious manner at the end. The twenty-two-year-old girl's murder may have been the culmination of all the angst and turmoil that had caused them to go on a spree of serial rapes and assaults lasting almost three months.

Deputy District Attorney Angela Backers stated in court that the couple intended to create a name for themselves. It was only a matter of time until they murdered someone;

and unfortunately, Vanessa Samson was the one they went for. According to Backers, the evidence recovered signified that Daveggio and Michaud had already decided that their next victim was not going to be let off since the authorities were closing in and their desire to kill was at its peak.

The serial raping and killing of James Anthony Daveggio and Michelle Lyn Michaud surpassed everything that the law enforcement agencies and crime experts believed to be true. Their history and troubled background is testimony to the fact that they both should have been behind bars much earlier in life or at least within the walls of a psychiatric facility. While Michaud did not draw any attention to herself during her adulthood, Daveggio managed to raise red flags on numerous occasions. It was by coincidence and strategy that he escaped the sex offender alert. His partner, on the other hand, did not show up as a suspect in criminal activity until much later.

Unabashedly, they continued to play out their relationship fantasies, eventually going from living in a house to moving around constantly in their minivan. Michaud remained a mystery which slowly began to unravel in the end as everything began to fall apart for the couple.

Experts and analysts debated over what bonded the two together so strongly. In the beginning of their relationship, it seemed as if the two was another one of those 'opposites attract' pairings. One was a rugged gang member who rode around on a stolen Harley-Davidson, the other, a sophisticated prostitute with a certain command over the spoken language. Experts noted that what was interesting about Michaud was the fact that she did not flaunt her line of work by her appearance or social behavior. For an onlooker, she might have been a conservative, middle-class woman reaching for the American dream.

Unlike her boyfriend, Michaud could engage people without raising any alarms. While Daveggio made constant grammatical errors and slurred his sentences, Michaud's conversational skills were top notch, and rarely did she make mistakes with her grammar. Later on, it was suggested that the two became close due to the sexual nature of their relationship. According to FBI profilers, sexual desire and gratification can be a pivotal factor in any relationship, particularly if it's between two budding criminals.

Psychological experts have found another fascinating development in the early lives of both Daveggio and Michaud. During their respective teen years, it was quite a role reversal. As per his fellow high school classmates, James Anthony Daveggio came across as a polite boy with deep blue eyes, which made it easier for the girls to trust him. Michaud, on the other hand, was a striking contradiction. She was abrasive, rebellious and did not have many friends either in school or around the neighborhood. It was the boy who was covering his underlying sociopathic tendencies at the time, while the girl displayed no inhibitions whatsoever. Young Michaud's indiscretions were already known and heard of by every acquaintance and family member.

Later on, both Daveggio and Michaud took on different personalities, hence prompting the debate that they were harboring a multiple personality disorder. It was Daveggio whose violence and aggression resulted in frequent brawls with his fellow schoolboys, causing public concern. Michaud somehow managed to rein in her rebellion and take on the portrayal of a relatively friendly woman. She built a relationship with her mother, even going on shopping trips and to restaurants, just like any other mother-daughter relationship.

The murderous killer that had been lurking inside Daveggio was threatening to come out. Even though Daveggio had kept a lid on that side of his personality, it was always clawing at him. During the investigation into his background, the authorities implied that, as a youngster, he might have been responsible for the assault on Cassie Riley that claimed her young life.

Furthermore, it was discovered that Daveggio could be linked to a few other unsolved murders and rapes. His police records showed that he had pleaded guilty to a couple of offenses as well. It was surprising that, despite his deteriorating mental stability, the psychiatric evaluation had concluded that nothing was wrong with him. There were a few experts and analysts who said that Daveggio's reports were clear because he was not psychologically ill at the time. He had been intent on acting out the sexual fantasies his mind conjured as the urges became overwhelming, fueled by Ihde's presence in his life.

Serial rapist and murderer Michael Ihde was caught and convicted after claiming the lives of innocent victims, much like his friend, James Anthony Daveggio. When Michaud came into his life, she was far from a calming influence. After the two began dating, his violent demeanor and aggression proceeded to worsen instead of subsiding.

There was no way to go but downwards for the both of them. Daveggio began to project his desires and twisted fantasies upon Michaud. Soon enough, she gave in and followed him. While Michaud might have been initially working out of the desire to salvage their relationship, Daveggio aimed for a serial killer partnership similar to Gerald and Charlene Gallego. However, neither one managed to achieve anything that they had in mind. Michelle Michaud spiraled down a path of darkness and cruelty while Daveggio became the other half of a deadly team who terrorized innocent young girls across California and Nevada.

Crime experts began to search for a possible trigger that might have led to their sudden recklessness with Samson. Before murdering her, they had let all their victims go. While the police closing in was a huge factor behind the couple's acceleration, analysts believe there was a psychological aspect to it as well. They had been raping and assaulting their victims for almost two months, toying with the idea of murder. Once they came to Pleasanton, California, Daveggio believed that it would be the ideal place for their first kill. He had grown up and spent most of his life in this town, and it was like coming full circle for him.

For Michaud, the situation had transgressed. By now, she was deriving pleasure in the acts of violence, and murder seemed the likely next step in her thrill-seeking spree. Michaud had become brazen and overconfident that they would never be caught. As the two maneuvered around the authorities, it did appear as if the two would manage to continue their terrorizing journey onward.

Thankfully, that did not happen and the police apprehended them. Neither Michaud nor Daveggio could have imagined that their first murder victim would also be their last. After Vanessa Samson, they had no intention of stopping. Yet, despite their best efforts to evade jail and long term arrest, it was all over.

Surprisingly, it was Michaud who gave away critical information linking both her and Daveggio to Samson's kidnapping and subsequent death. Law enforcement officials already feared that Daveggio and Michaud were behind this heinous crime, but they did not have any certainty of proof. It wasn't until Michaud broke down in prison upon watching the news report and confessed to her cellmate that she was in 'trouble,' that the detectives and FBI agents discovered the truth. The fact that it was Michaud who succumbed first under pressure was quite an unusual development in the case. Up till now, she had been the one in control and in charge of the situation. It was not like her to relent or display weakness, particularly when things were looking so dire.

Perhaps the reason that she broke was that she realized it was the end. They were not going to get away with their crimes anymore. She had been isolated from her partner and it was all over for the two of them. This could have triggered her turmoil and caused her enough distress to divulge information regarding Samson. Experts could argue that Michaud's confession may have even been spurred by guilt. She was caught and in prison; all the doors were closing in on her, and she knew that it was not going to end well for her. Hence, when she heard that Vanessa Samson had been found dead, the guilt of her actions overwhelmed her.

However, that is one far-fetched theory. The popular opinion about Michelle Michaud is that there wasn't a guilty or remorseful bone in her body. She did not feel regret for anything she had done. When the police caught and arrested Daveggio and Michaud for rape and assault, the only thing that concerned her was finding a way out. She did not intend to stay in prison for long and wanted to be out as soon as possible. Her previous encounters with the police had led her to believe that there was a possibility of serving a short-term sentence and securing release.

Experts and profilers believe that when she saw the news report and deduced that the police were conducting an investigation into Samson's murder, she knew that it could implicate her. According to her cellmate, Michaud started to cry and then admitted that something was gravely wrong. All of a sudden, the woman who had expressed no emotion as yet was breaking down. However, it was all momentary. The police and investigators claimed that she seemed to give up information readily during the interviews. Experts tried to explain her behavior from various aspects.

Many thought that she wanted redemption, while others believed that it was another ploy. Michaud was either trying to throw clues to the police that would only lead them to Daveggio, or she wanted a deal in exchange for helping the police with the murder investigation. Perhaps she had convinced herself that there was still a way for her to get ahead. It appeared that Michaud had become so distant from reality that she could not gauge what was happening around her.

After a day of interviewing, the police officers and detectives had already reached the conclusion that Michaud and her partner, Daveggio, were Samson's murderers.

However, Michaud still seemed oblivious to the fact that her story was over. There was not going to be the ending that she wanted or hoped for. Michaud had admitted to the truth and she would never be able to retreat from it.

If she did admit to the information herself, it would not be that much of a shock. The woman's mind was a mystery to everyone. She was a bold and dominant woman who believed that she did not have to adhere to any rules. Psychological experts believe that she was so wrapped up in her own sense of superiority that by divulging the information to the investigating officials, she may have been trying to gain some lost ground.

There are others who opine that Michaud took pride in her actions, which is perhaps why she admitted her involvement in Samson's murder. On a previous occasion, when she saw Juanita Rodriguez's incident being reported on TV, she proudly boasted about it in front of her daughter and Nancy Baker. In her statement, the young girl went on record to say that when she was at Daveggio and Michaud's house and the details regarding Juanita Rodriguez's abduction and rape were reported, she heard Michaud announce, "We did that."

While initially Michaud may have been inclined to reveal the information regarding Samson, she changed her stance completely as the investigation was handed over to federal authorities. She did not shy away from trying everything she could to get away.

There was no doubt that the woman was devious, sociopathic and devoid of any moral fiber which could cause her to exercise some humanity. During the trial, her statements were also used to charge and convict Daveggio. The two were separated at last, but not without wreaking havoc and causing long-lasting trauma to their victims. A young innocent life that was full of hopes and dreams for the future was lost.

While the death penalty may have come as justice being served at the end, it would do little to fill the void that Vanessa Samson's death left in the lives of her loved ones. She caught the eye of the deadly demons on her way to work, but unlike their previous victims, she did not get to escape.

Both Daveggio and Michaud were overtaken by a strong desire to kill and they knew that the timing was perfect with the holidays settling in. Samson was their last victim and one who will be remembered as one of the most brutal murders in America's serial crime history.

Appreciation

Thank you to my editor, proofreaders, and cover artist for your support:

Aeternum Designs (book cover); Bettye McKee (editor); Katherine McCarthy, Robyn MacEachern, Kathi Garcia, Sandra Miller, Tracey Dearlove, Lee Husemann

~ RJ

Enjoy this book? You can make a big difference.

Reviews are one of the most powerful tools when it comes to book ranking, exposure and future sales. I have a bunch of loyal readers, and honest reviews of my books help bring them to the attention of other readers.

If you've enjoyed this book, I would be very grateful if you'd take a few minutes to write a brief review on Amazon.

Thank you so much,

RJ

Books by RJ Parker

Parents Who Killed Their Children: True stories of Filicide, Mental Health and Postpartum Psychosis

Serial Homicide: Notorious Serial Killers: (4 Books in Series)

Abduction

Top Cases of the FBI: Volumes I and II

The Basement

Forensic Analysis and DNA in Criminal Investigations and Cold Cases Solved: True Crime Stories

Serial Killers Encyclopedia: The Encyclopedia of Serial Killers from A to Z

Social Media Monsters: Killers Who Target Victims on the Internet

Escaped Killer

Revenge Killings

Killing the Rainbow

Marc Lépine: True Story of the Montreal Massacre: School Shootings

Backseat Tragedies: Hot Car Deaths

Women Who Kill

Beyond Stick and Stones

Cold Blooded Killers

Case Closed: Serial Killers Captured

Radical Islamic Terrorism in America Today

Hell's Angels Biker War

Serial Killer Groupies

Serial Killer Case Files

Blood Money: The Method and Madness of Assassins: Stories of Real Contract Killers

Serial Killers True Crime Anthologies: Volumes 1 – 4

About the Author

RJ Parker, Ph.D., is an award-winning and bestselling true crime author and owner of RJ Parker Publishing, Inc. He has written over 30 true crime books which are available in eBook, paperback and audiobook editions, and have sold in over 100 countries. He holds certifications in Serial Crime, Criminal Profiling and a Ph.D. in Criminology.

To date, RJ has donated over 3,000 autographed books to allied troops serving overseas and to our wounded warriors recovering in Naval and Army hospitals all over the world. He also donates to Victims of Violent Crimes Canada.

Contact Information

Author's Email:
AuthorRJParker@gmail.com
Publisher's Email:
Agent@RJParkerPublishing.com
Website:
http://RJPARKERPUBLISHING.com/
Twitter:
http://www.Twitter.com/realRJParker
Facebook:
https://www.Facebook.com/AuthorRJParker
Instagam:
https://Instagram.com/RJParkerPub
Bookbub:
https://www.bookbub.com/authors/rj-parker
Amazon Author's Page:
rjpp.ca/RJ-PARKER-BOOKS

Made in United States
North Haven, CT
31 May 2022